How to Make Your Audience
Fall in Love with You

If you have a home computer with Internet access you may:
- request an item to be placed on hold.
- renew an item that is not overdue or on hold.
- view titles and due dates checked out on your card.
- view and/or pay your outstanding fines online (over $5).

To view your patron record from your home computer click on Patchogue-Medford Library's homepage: **www.pmlib.org**

How to Make Your Audience Fall in Love with You

Expert Advice on Acting Technique, Script Analysis, and *Taking Risks*

Deryn Warren

HEINEMANN ■ Portsmouth, NH

Heinemann
361 Hanover Street
Portsmouth, NH 03801–3912
www.heinemanndrama.com

Offices and agents throughout the world

Library of Congress Cataloging-in-Publication Data
Warren, Deryn.
  How to make your audience fall in love with you : expert advice on acting technique, script analysis, and taking risks / Deryn Warren.
      p. cm.
  ISBN-13: 978-0-325-01393-0
  ISBN-10: 0-325-01393-4
  1. Acting.   I. Title.
  PN2061.W35 2008
  792.02'8—dc22   2008017747

Editor: Maura Sullivan
Production coordinator: Elizabeth Valway
Production service: Matrix Productions Inc.
Typesetter: Eisner/Martin Typographics
Cover design: Joni Doherty
Manufacturing: Steve Bernier

Printed in the United States of America on acid-free paper
12 11 10 09 08 VP 1 2 3 4 5

To my children, Alexander (Pie) Griffiths, Rachel Griffiths, Maria Springer, Sophie Springer, and Luke Springer; and to my siblings, Leslie Sarn, Christopher Warren, Gillian Smith, and Kevin Warren and their spouses; and of course the cousins; and Pat Price and family; and Sirie and Jay Palmos; and the Fullers; and the adopted members; and the entire huge extended Warren family of which I am so happy to be a part.

Contents

Acknowledgments

No author could have a better experience with a publishing house than I had with Heinemann. I want to thank everyone I worked with there: Managing Editor Maura Sullivan, Production Editor Elizabeth Valway, and Acquisitions Editor Cheryl Kimball, who was so kind and helpful. Editorial Coordinator Stephanie Turner and I agreed to overlook each other's typos on the countless emails we sent back and forth; I feel I have a new long-distance friend. Aaron Downey of Matrix Productions Inc., calmed me down and explained the editing system with humor and expertise and later changed the most minute details with continued humor and grace. Kate Petrella has to be the best copyeditor in the business, as her suggestions were brilliant and she caught things no one else could possibly have seen. Eric Chalek, the copywriter at Heinemann, worked with me generously and patiently and was as terrific as the rest of this expert and fun group of people. Thank you also to Jean Schiffman for introducing me to Heinemann. Last, I thank the former Heinemann Acquisitions Editor, Lisa Barnett, who encouraged me even as she was losing her battle with cancer. I won't forget you, Lisa.

I also want to thank my family and friends who read the manuscript and gave me encouragement and advice. Thank you Rachel Griffiths, Sophie and Maria Springer, John Griffiths, Bina Breitner, Robin Hiller-Fuller, Catherine Clinch, Laura Olson, and editor Charlotte Hildebrand, who gave suggestions for the structure. And thank you to Twink Caplan and Larry Hankin for their advice to actors.

*I*ntroduction

Early in my career I was looking for a middle-aged German man to play the part of an elevator operator for a play I was directing in Los Angeles. A young African American man sent a résumé with a note saying he knew he wasn't right for the role, but he wanted to audition anyway. I couldn't resist his enterprise (in those days I was doing my own casting), so I put him on the list. The producers and I had finished auditioning many competent but unexciting middle-aged actors with German accents when the young man came in to read for us. As soon as he began we were in love. He was charming, funny, and appealing. Without lines he showed exactly what he thought of everyone who got in the elevator. He brought so much more to the role than I or the writer had dreamed was possible that we rewrote the part for him.

Since then I have watched hundreds of actors audition, but less than one in twenty made everyone in the room say, "Bingo! That actor brought something so unexpected and remarkable to the role that he's got the part."

I wrote this book to make you that actor. Whether you're in a casting room, on stage, in film, or in television, whether you're doing Shakespeare, a sitcom, or a soap opera, I want you to be a better actor than you dreamed was possible. I will show you how to risk, how to go beyond the obvious, and how to use your most exciting self in every role. You will learn to make the best out of every script, deepen your choices, perfect your technique, and get hired. Once you have the job, you will make your audience fall in love with you.

1 Ways to Make the Audience (and the Casting Director) Fall in Love with You

Use Yourself, Not a "Character"

We want to see your unique self, not your unique self's *idea* of a character.

You are different from everyone else. Your parents, your history, culture, friendships, traumas, socioeconomic status, and education all add up to give you a rich background to draw upon. Each actor's approach to the circumstances of a role is different. If you use yourself, you are using your rich background.

No matter how much background material you could imagine for your "character," no matter how many pages of background you write, your imaginary character will never match your long and complicated history. Use *yourself* in the *circumstances* of the role. It is *you* who are in love. *You* are robbing a bank. *You* have only one eye. Use your imagination about the circumstances, but use yourself and *your* instincts to react.

If you are playing someone with a low I.Q., play yourself having a low-I.Q. moment. We all have times when we can't figure out a math problem, or can't read a map. We feel silly or embarrassed or we laugh at ourselves. Make sure it is *you* working to understand something that is beyond you. There is nothing interesting about playing a dumb person with no dimensions. *You* embarrassed that you are not smart, *you* working to understand what is beyond you, or *you* trying to cover up that you don't understand, are all interesting choices that involve hard work.

We all play many roles in daily life: employee, parent, lover, friend, party animal, and professional person. In each role we act differently, but we are still the same person. You will feel different in every role, just as you feel different when you are wearing a formal outfit compared to when you are wearing jeans. That is why it has been said that a costume is 80 percent of a character. We assume roles all the time and we are ourselves in each one of them.

Assume a role, but *don't* play a character. Be yourself in the situation with your own reactions. I call it **looking out of your own eyes**.

No matter what role you play—a superhero, a supermodel, an intellectual, a farmer, or even a psychopath, you want your audience to be thinking, "That actor is so exciting, intelligent, and full of vitality that I'm falling in love."

How do you make them love you?

Risk!

For every audition and for every scene, never be content with just saying the lines with some kind of meaning and emotion. Anyone off the street can do that. Risk! Add to the scene the biggest gift you have— yourself. Not your everyday self, but your extraordinary self.

Have you heard a recording of Martin Luther King Jr.'s "I have a dream" speech? You could read his powerful words and be moved, but when you hear him saying the words using all his passion, his thunderous voice, his care to make each phrase of great consequence, then you are stirred and changed. He risked because he wanted to make an impact. He wanted to change the world.

Why do actors so often work with only a third of their personality showing? Without their natural energy and humor? Without even using their full voice? So many actors whisper, as if they were doing commercials for personal hygiene products. Polite is boring. Playing it safe is boring. Taking chances, risking, extending an idea from safe to spectacular is the actor's mission.

Actors risk by using all of *themselves*, their own passion, humor, charm, intelligence, and vitality, by making unconventional choices and by not being afraid to make fools of themselves.

Two actors play the part of a bank robber. The first actor commands men, women, and children to sit on the floor and not move. He sounds like a mean cop ordering around criminals he despises. He threatens to blow them all to hell if they give him any trouble. Then he grabs the money and runs.

The next actor is just as tough but *even though he has the same lines*, he uses a flirtatious tone when he talks to the women. His eyes widen with glee when he sees the money. He even winks at a scared kid.

Yes. He's the actor the casting director will cast. He's the actor the audience will fall in love with because he is the actor relating to the other actors in the scene, using all of his personality: his humor, pleasure in life, and confidence.

At parties, do we notice the person who sits in a corner not disturbing anyone? No. Going to a party determined to have a good time takes a get-up-and-go attitude and guts. We notice the person who is fascinated or amused by the other guests. Why would actors choose to be any less?

Even though Hannibal Lector, played so brilliantly by Anthony Hopkins in *The Silence of the Lambs*, was a serial killer, we found him mesmerizing. He used irony, which is a dark humor, and exhibited a fierce intelligence. Look at *The West Wing*. There isn't a scene in which the actors don't use irony or a wry sense of the ridiculous. The men on the staff like each other. They have fun. They look like people you'd like to meet. It's how they got the parts.

Some people can sit in a chair not saying anything and they look appealing. "I bet that man has a lot to say. I want to meet him," you might think. You are attracted to his interest in his surroundings, a twinkle in his eye, an appreciation of the people around him. Jack Nicholson just has to raise an eyebrow and the audience adores him. He takes a lot of pleasure in himself. He always looks happy and cool, and his raised eyebrow tells you he's having a fantastic time. He may not look as good as he used to, but he's just as engaging and fun.

George Clooney, Goldie Hawn, Cuba Gooding Jr., Jackie Chan, Hugh Grant, and Will Smith all have charm and humor too. Their personalities made them stars.

You don't have to be in a comedy or even have an outgoing personality to win over an audience. The vulnerability of shy people, an ability to laugh at themselves, and the energy it takes for them to fit in is very appealing. The point is that you should never use an excuse not to show as much of yourself as possible. No actor should say, "I'm playing a nun. I have no feelings for men." Or, "I'm a lawyer. I have to behave professionally at all times." These excuses don't allow your personality to reveal itself. Using excuses, *inexperienced actors rationalize why they don't have to risk.* Actors tell me "I wouldn't do that" when the role they are playing demands more than they feel comfortable with, but we don't want to see only your everyday persona. We want to see the part of you that is capable of being a hero, or of being cruel, or of showing exquisite tenderness. We want you to have depth.

You have to push your comfort level. I once coached an actor who was auditioning for the part of a bomb expert defusing a bomb with the clock ticking. She said the words just fine, but her body wasn't tense. She couldn't raise the stakes high enough. She didn't put herself in the situation. In the scene she was in mortal danger, but she was afraid to make a fool of herself by "overacting." How could anyone believe she was defusing a bomb that was about to go off, if her body didn't show extreme tension? (She didn't get the part.)

A new student in my class had not yet learned to use all of her personality. Her first line said she was tired, so she played weary throughout the scene, which is not attractive. She needed to play a game of humorously being soooo tired instead. She argued with her male partner, making points in an irritated fashion, and even went so far as to sigh at his lack of understanding. No one would find such a person appealing. When I suggested she work to make him fall in love with her instead of merely scoring points, she was transformed. She became sexy, intelligent, likable, and humorous. The argument became a playful flirtation. We liked her (and the scene) because she showed us many aspects of herself.

Dare to be dramatic. Dare to stand out from the crowd. Dare to make risky choices. It's how you got your first part over the competition and how you keep getting parts.

Always Use Humor

Risk by using humor in places that are not obvious. A sense of humor makes actors so appealing that it should be a part of every role. Even drama should have humor. Not necessarily the "hah hah" kind, but at least a wry acknowledgment of the oddness of the situation. A small laugh can escape in tense situations. For example, I was in a hospital waiting room while my mother was having a heart operation. Another family was there to support a young woman in her thirties whose husband was dying. At one point her friend brought in a huge platter of assorted sandwiches and told the young wife she needed to eat. The wife looked over the platter and gave a slight laugh as she wondered how to choose between so many. In the midst of tragedy there was still humor, which released the tension of the room. It was very human. If it had been an audition, the laugh would have added a unique dimension that might have sealed the part. (But again, don't do anything for the casting director or audience; only concentrate on what you are doing to or for your partner in the scene, and use your natural instincts.)

Playing games with lines or using sarcasm are other important aspects of humor. One actor whines, "I'm so tired." The other actor says the same words but sinks dramatically into a chair with the back of her hand on her forehead. She's playing a game. They both may *be* tired, but which one is more appealing to his partner in the scene, and which one would the casting director fall for?

Look at the following lines.

                              LUKE
    Brilliant speech, Max. Pithy lines. Pure
    genius.

                              MAX
    What do you want?

Luke isn't giving Max a real compliment. Luke is playing the game of—I'll give you a ridiculously flowery pseudo-compliment, and you'll know I want something. The exchange should amuse them both.

Game-playing makes unbearable situations bearable. Look at these lines from the title characters of *Thelma & Louise*, who are on the run for murder and are about to commit suicide by driving their car off a cliff.

> THELMA
> I guess everything we've got to lose is already gone anyway.

> LOUISE
> How do you stay so positive?

We love courageous people using humor in the face of disaster.

One of my students doing a cold reading in class had a line asking her partner for a small favor. When he agreed, she said, "Really?" and laughed with so much pleasure and surprise that she got a laugh from us. What an unexpected, risky, and delightful choice for such an insignificant line.

The lesson is to find some aspect of humor in every role and to use yourself and all of your best assets—your intelligence and vitality—to achieve your goals with your partner.

Another way to make your audience love you:

Use Energy

Energy is attractive.

Energy is full of life.

Energy is sexy.

Energy draws attention.

Energy makes stars.

Energy is fun.

Too many actors are so terrified of overacting that they underact, and no one notices them. They justify their boring performances by believing that using energy and making risky choices won't make them seem "natural." But natural is often boring. If you are in a restaurant waiting for a friend to arrive, and you're idly listening to the conversation of a couple next to you, you will find that nine times out of ten it won't interest you. Everyday life may be "natural," but it is not the stuff of drama.

Don't be afraid of overacting. We do it in real life. We overreact to things that later we realize were not important. We get furious, impassioned, and strident. We fight for our political views and maybe offend people with opposite views. Haven't you ever been accused of going too far on some occasion? Overreacting is fascinating. Don't we strain to overhear a couple fighting in a parking lot, and don't we stop dead in the street to grin at someone whooping with happiness?

If a woman breaks a nail she can look at it with indifference and figure it will grow out, or she might go nuts. "Oh no! I had a perfect set of nails. The prom is tonight! This is an *emergency!*" There is no limit to how excited a woman can get about that fingernail, and the indifferent woman and the overexcited one can both be believable. Acting is about making choices. Exciting, energetic choices. Raise the stakes. Make that broken fingernail a disaster!

Melodrama is faking large emotion. If you don't fake, you'll be believed.

You will never be accused of overacting if afterwards you apologize in the scene with a smile or laugh at yourself or are embarrassed. Scenes should go up and down in energy, not stay steady. Steady will put the audience to sleep.

I went to a concert at Royce Hall in Los Angeles with a full orchestra and four cellists ranked in order of skill from first down to fourth. Three of the cellists leaned forward as they played. The fourth and least important cellist relaxed against the back of his chair. Each cellist concentrated. They were all excellent and skilled musicians. They all played the correct notes, but the fourth cellist didn't have that extra something . . . energy.

Passive actors, actors who wait for their partners to begin the scene, who wait for their partner's long speech to be over without itching to jump in and say something, who don't have passion, are boring. They aren't working hard. They're using a disappointing fraction of their energy.

> **TIP:** *In any scene the actor with the most energy is the one the audience notices the most, even if that actor has fewer lines.*

Another word for energy is WORK. Even if you don't have lines, you must be working hard. The work of a scene involves giving your partner a message. You send messages throughout the whole scene through your lines and your actions. Hard work is interesting to watch. I don't mean the work of preparing for a scene; I mean the work expended when one actor is working with passion to change his partner. When he has no lines he is still sending specific silent messages. He is concentrating, focused, energetic, ardent, fervent, and therefore fascinating. During a political debate, the panelists up on the stage waiting to speak are still using energy to react to what is being said, to comment with laughter or scorn or by shaking their heads. They are energized and communicative even without words. Their energy draws attention.

Work does not necessarily involve talk. Imagine going out with a new lover. You are constantly touching, flirting, giving sexy looks, turning your partner on, and showing your partner your appreciation. All this takes *work*. Think of a mother telling her child silently with a look or a gesture to kiss Aunt Mary—the Aunt Mary with a bristly moustache. The message is clear to the child. If it's a comedy, the harder the mom *works* to send the message to the unwilling child, the louder the laughs will be.

Work is not necessarily loud. Filled silences take work. How about the silence after a marriage proposal, when the man wills the woman to accept? A lion hunkered down in the grass, concentrating on his prey, waiting to spring, is working hard. A couple giving each other a sexually charged look, or a soldier squinting down the barrel of his rifle, are all at their most alive. Their muscles are tight. They are focused and engaged. Work!

> **TIP:** *If your stomach muscles aren't tight, you're not using enough energy. You're not working hard enough.*

Don't think about tightening your stomach muscles. Work harder on changing your partner, and your muscles will tighten automatically. When I am talking to my students in class, my muscles are always tight and I sit up straight in my chair. Why? Because I care about them and I am working hard to communicate. If you are focused, your muscles will be working.

Love Yourself

Casting directors and audiences love actors who love themselves.

Did you ever see a skinny guy flex his muscles proudly in front of a mirror? Didn't it make you laugh? Sure, it's funny that he pretends he is gorgeous and ripped when he's not, but our biggest enjoyment comes from his taking so much pleasure in himself. He's being silly and having fun, and that makes us have fun. It makes us like him.

Don't we love a kid who scores a goal and comes running off the field flushed with pride and pleasure? Don't we laugh at his pleasure? Isn't that kid the most appealing person in the crowd at that moment?

Conceit doesn't look appealing. It looks self-involved. But confidence, readiness to laugh, and a great sense of humor are all very appealing. Look for places in your scenes where you can add these upbeat traits. Even Hannibal Lector, tied up and in a cell, still enjoyed his own brilliance.

I see actors make the choice to whine throughout their scenes, or become shrill, or shuffle back and forth, or hide behind their hair. Why should your partner do what you want if you are showing him such unattractive traits? Love yourself enough to make attractive choices for your partner.

Summary

Use your own passion, quirkiness, strength, intelligence, confidence, and depth. The more aspects you show us of yourself, the more riveting the audience will find you. Always find the humor or irony in every scene. Work with passion, focus, and energy to change your partner, and you've got the part. (Well, you have the part if you look the part, or their idea of it. If you aren't too young or too old, too fat or too thin, too tall or too short, or if the director's girlfriend doesn't get it. This business is tough, but you knew that.)

2 Making Choices, or What Am I Fighting For?

Paradoxically, in order to get the casting director and the audience to love you, you must pay no attention to what they are thinking while you work. You must only pay attention to your partner in the scene. Every scene is about you fighting to change your partner in some way. This fight is the first building block of acting. Teachers call it by many different names, such as Intention, Action, Motivation, or Goal. I like the term "Fighting For," used by Michael Shurtleff, who wrote *Audition,* because it implies the strongest conflict. The more you need the change from your partner, the harder you will fight. The higher the stakes and the more you care about winning, the more riveting the scene will be.

Take a scene in which a man on a treadmill is trying to pick up a stunning woman on the machine next to him. You might say he is *just* Fighting to have sex with her or to get a date with her. This is a minimal and obvious choice that doesn't have complications or layers or importance. Make him have to Fight extra hard. Raise the stakes! Make it the first woman he's asked out in a year. Make him gay and trying to be straight. Make him so lonely that he'll kill himself if this woman won't agree to date him. Too many actors do just what is written on the page. Risky choices give extra fascinating layers to the scene.

Here are some choices you could make when you are working on scenes:

What Am I Fighting For?

To test my partner's commitment.

To win the game we are playing. (Make sure to register wins and losses.)

To be perfect for my partner. Or to be exactly what I think my partner wants me to be.

To change my partner's mind.

To make my partner crazy.

To inspire my partner to do something I want.

To seek revenge on my partner.

To make my partner fall in love with me.

To force my partner to see my point of view.

To prove to my partner I am good enough (for his family, a job, or whatever may be at stake.)

To prove to my partner I am better than he/she is.

To get my partner to do what I want and *like* it.

To change my partner into the person I want him/her to be.

To maintain the status quo in the relationship (because you are terrified of change, so the stakes are high).

To punish my partner.

Notice that *all the goals involve your partner in the scene*. If you are arguing with your brother about whether to put your mother in a home, don't make the argument about your mother; make it a power struggle between you and your brother. Scenes are always about changing your partner, not a third party. Always make sure you are enmeshed with your partner even if the scene is about someone or something else.

Metaphorically lean forward in your eagerness to change your partner. Don't make weak choices like getting your partner to like you. We all want everyone to like us, so that is not strong enough or interesting enough.

There are infinite choices for Fighting Fors. The previous list offers only a few suggestions. When you make *your* choice as to what to Fight For, make sure it is a choice with high stakes. Remember that all your choices should be urgent enough that your stomach muscles are tight—a surefire indicator that you are working hard enough toward the important goal that you chose. Your choice should feel like an invisible hand on the front of your shirt pulling you toward your goal of changing your partner.

Look at the Fighting For "To be perfect for my partner." This goal could be useful for a scene in which you find yourself with a dangerous crazy person. Every muscle in your body is poised to jump out of harm's way. Your brain is racing to find the best way to talk to this person. You are on high alert. No one will be able to take their eyes off you.

The Fighting For "To be perfect for my partner" could also involve a wife with a tyrannical husband. She meekly tries not to infuriate her husband. She brings him food and agrees with his opinions. But it must be hard work to *act* so passive, when she's not naturally passive, and we should see the toll it takes on her. Imagine if you had to cater to your mate's every whim. But make sure you don't lose your sense of humor or irony when you play this part. You could be plotting to kill him. You could be having an affair under his nose. There must be flashes of your old independent self. If you don't use your strong self in the role, and your dislike of being meek, then you will be in danger of seeming dull, dull, dull. Remember, you have to use as many aspects of yourself as you can in every scene.

Look at the goal of "To test my partner's commitment." Don't we all do that in romantic relationships? We put our partners in situations like meeting the in-laws to see how they do. We may pick fights to see if they will love us anyway. We may push for marriage to test whether they are serious. Children press their parents all the time to see what they can get away with.

The Fighting For of "To win the game we are playing" could involve a couple arguing over which restaurant they are going to. If the exchange is lighthearted it can be fun, but of course the issue of control looms large. Another game-playing Fighting For could be about neatness. "Honey," the wife could say, "your sock is on the bathroom floor. It's lonely for its partner." The husband replies that the sock is happy where it is. This is a game, but again the conflict is real and can go deep. All game-playing is a light way of dealing with real issues.

Sarcasm is a game. What if a woman expects her lover to greet her with flowers and he appears with one rose hastily plucked from the garden? Instead of getting furious, she uses game-playing, saying "You sure went all out," which makes the same point. Her Fighting For is to make her husband be more romantic—or else!

> **TIP:** *Look for lines in your scripts that could be played with games.*

There is a scene in *Seinfeld* in which Kramer wants Jerry to taste a piece of cantaloupe and Jerry doesn't want to. It's a silly but funny argument. After Jerry reluctantly tastes the cantaloupe and rather likes it, Kramer tells Jerry that he should buy all his fruit at Joe's instead of the shop he goes to. Again Jerry resists, and gives Kramer reasons why the closer shop is better.

What is Kramer Fighting For? There are several choices from the previous list: to force Jerry to see his point of view; to get Jerry to do what Kramer wants; or to change Jerry into the person Kramer wants him to be, i.e., a cantaloupe-eating, smart shopper.

Kramer must care desperately that Jerry eat the cantaloupe. He doesn't let up on him. When he wins and Jerry takes a bite, Kramer Fights to get Jerry to say it's the best he ever ate. Then he wants Jerry to shop where he shops. The further Kramer goes with his desire to change Jerry, the more fun it is.

Jerry has the harder part in this because he is reacting to Kramer. Jerry could be Fighting to win the game they are playing—the game of Kramer insisting and Jerry resisting. Or Jerry could Fight to keep Kramer from running his life. But don't forget that this is a comedy, and Jerry's energy and commitment have to match Kramer's. Jerry should not fall into the trap of being negative and down. For example, when he finally tastes the cantaloupe he should say that it's very good with pleasure and surprise, not grudgingly.

This scene is a wonderful example of topping. After Kramer makes a point, Jerry has to top him with a better point, and then Kramer has to top *him* with even *more* fervor. Each actor tops the other, and the energy rises as the contest continues. Because this is a light comedy, each actor's last line should have an up-tilt. Don't let the last words go downward and drag the comedic energy down.

TIP: *Always end a comedic audition or a scene with up energy. Never let the last words run downhill. Win the last point. Or if you can't win, at least be prepared to try with that same up energy.*

If your last line in a light comedy is, for example, "I think you should leave," then don't say it with disgust, with the word *leave* going down in energy. Say, "I think you should *leave!*" with up energy, as if leaving is the best idea you can think of. This way your Fighting For is still strong, but the comedic approach is still there.

Fighting Fors Without Words

Don't forget that words are only a fraction of the message. Sending specific messages with silent dialogue is just as important. There are many ways other than words to change your partner.

1. Body language. Gestures of impatience, intimate loving touches, snarls, sniffs of superiority, kisses of all types, downturns of the mouth signifying disapproval; all of these are wordless messages.
2. Physical violence. If you are fighting verbally, add blows to the scene and watch the stakes rise. (If you are auditioning, you must choreograph the blows with your partner. If that is not possible, hit the furniture instead.)
3. Looks. Looks are potent. What could be a more powerful message than rolling eyes, or eyes brimming with tears and reproach? Or a look of disgust from a wife to a husband flirting at a party? Looks can tell your partner "I find you attractive," "You hurt my feelings," "You are sexy," "You make me sick," "I'm warning you!" "You're boring me," "You think *that's* interesting?" "I love you," or "You're funny." Silent messages are often more effective than words.

TIP: *The camera itches to do a close-up if an actor is conveying silent messages.*

Find Your Partner Worthy of the Fight

Never find your partner uninteresting. If you find your partner dull, then you are in danger of appearing dull. Find your partner infuriating or sinful or evil or gross, but don't ever find him not worth your effort. Never choose that you want your partner to leave the room. Choose that you want him to stay so you can score points or make him miserable. You can *tell* him you want him to leave, but don't *really* want him to. What fun would you have then?

The opposite of love is not anger or hate; it is indifference. If you are indifferent to your partner, we don't have a spellbinding scene. You must care enough about your partner to be angry with him. If you are fighting, then the more involved you are with your partner in the scene, the higher the stakes are, and the angrier you will be.

> **TIP:** *Your Fighting For is always to actively and passionately work to change your partner, who is always worth the huge effort.*

Picking the wrong Fighting For can adversely affect your scene. Two men in my class did a scene, and one of them appeared weak in comparison to his partner. The weak one was Fighting For his partner to save him. In another context that is a fine choice, but in this case, when the weaker actor chose instead to Fight to prove that he was equal to his partner, his performance was transformed. Choose a Fighting For that works best for your scene and that makes you work hard.

The following scene is from *The Lady and the Clarinet*, by Michael Christofer. Paul, who works for Luba's father, is picking up some papers. Luba is nervous about a date who is about to arrive. This scene can make actors fall into the **trap of indifference** to their partner.

What are Paul and Luba Fighting For?

PAUL: I should have telephoned first.
LUBA: Because I was a virgin.
PAUL: Just to see . . . what?
LUBA: I'm a virgin.
PAUL: Oh. Well, I'm sorry.
LUBA: Not half as sorry as I am. Oh God I wish I were dead. I wish I were dead and buried alive and forty years old . . . Are you still here?
PAUL: Yes, I think so.
LUBA: Look at you. Look at yourself. Look at your clothes. You've been wearing the same pair of pants since the day I was born. Where do you come from Paul?

```
PAUL:   Nowhere.
LUBA:   Perfect.
PAUL:   I mean I was born here.
LUBA:   Lived here all your life.
PAUL:   Oh, yes.
LUBA:   Yes. Perfectly happy here.
PAUL:   Oh, yes.
LUBA:   Never think you might shove your feeble life
        into a suitcase and just hit the road?
PAUL:   Why?
LUBA:   I don't know. Just for the hell of it. Don't
        you ever feel a need, a pull, a yearning to
        break loose, break out, tear down the walls
        and run? Christ, what are you made of? You
        have a destiny. Fate has plans for you. Why
        do you think God put you on this earth?
        You're here for a reason.
PAUL:   I just came for the papers.
LUBA:   Jesus, Mary and Joseph. Am I the only living
        thing alive?
PAUL:   What's the matter with you? You're all crazy.
LUBA:   I'm dying. I can feel it. Every cell in my body
        is screaming for air. My skin is suffocating.
PAUL:   Golly.
LUBA:   Yeah. Golly.
PAUL:   Maybe you should see . . .
LUBA:   What? A doctor?
PAUL:   Well . . .
```

If done literally, Paul's responses could make him appear as if he stupidly doesn't understand that Luba is implying he is limited and unsophisticated, when she asks if he has lived in one place all his life. What casting director or audience is interested in a stupid man? Just because Luba is implying that Paul is limited and unadventurous, don't fall into the trap of making him stupid and dull.

And don't fall into the trap of thinking Luba is not interested in him.

```
PAUL:   Oh, yes.
LUBA:   Yes. Perfectly happy here.
PAUL:   Oh, yes.
```

```
LUBA:  Never think you might shove your feeble life
       into a suitcase and just hit the road?
PAUL:  Why?
```

It seems at first glance that the character of Paul doesn't like Luba. After all, he thinks she is nuts and should see a doctor, so doesn't he want to get away as fast as possible? No! Remember, if you're indifferent to your partner, then *you* appear unattractive and boring and we don't have a scene worth watching. Choose that Paul is fascinated by Luba and the more she rants and raves, the more intrigued he gets. Perhaps he has a boring life and he's never heard anyone so open, emotional, and flamboyant. He's attracted to her and amused by her putting him down. *He* knows he's not dumb and provincial.

To make him attractive and interesting and *smart,* play that Paul is amused by her putting him down. He's teasing her. Look at Paul's response to the following lines:

```
LUBA:  Not half as sorry as I am. Oh God I wish I
       were dead. I wish I were dead and buried
       alive and forty years old . . . Are you
       still here?
PAUL:  Yes, I think so.
```

Paul is making a joke. He could laugh out loud with delight at this amazing woman.

When Luba says, "Jesus, Mary and Joseph. Am I the only living thing alive?" Paul says, "What's the matter with you?" but not in a nasty way. He asks with *genuine interest.*

So instead of the casting director seeing a disapproving, stupid, judgmental, sour-faced man, he will see a man with a sense of humor showing his appreciation of a beautiful woman and having a great time. Paul has never met anyone like her. Paul could be Fighting to be perfect for Luba, to be the kind of man she would want him to be. He has to struggle over his answers to make them just right. Read the scene again with that in mind.

You might also think that Luba dislikes Paul and is not interested in him, but Luba is Fighting to change Paul into a more exciting man. She goads him, embarrasses him, and forces him to look at himself. She has to think he is *worth* this big effort. Choose that she is as attracted to him as he is to her. Do this as a love scene instead of a mutual put-down scene and your audience will be enthralled.

Attractive Fighting Fors

Like the choices for Paul that made him look attractive instead of nasty and judgmental, be sure in every scene to make choices that make you fascinating to your partner (and your audience). Take the whine out of your voice. Don't act tired or bored. Don't make any of the choices that make you not like someone, or that make you look like a drag. I know a beautiful woman who is bitter, whiny, and has a victim complex. Although she is attentive to her dates, she is never asked out a second time. Take a lesson from her misfortunes and wherever possible, even if you are playing a killer, make attractive choices in your work. (In your life, too.)

I recently met a young actress at a hair salon. She was funny, full of character, and energetic. When I told her I was an acting teacher, she asked for some tips for a play she was rehearsing. I told her that the first line of any scene should have an action. She said her first lines were something like "Hey! I know what you did. You creep." She said them for me, running the three lines together and saying them nastily as if she were weary and disgusted. None of the charm or energy I had been taken with showed in her work. As she said the lines, her personal appeal was nil. No one would cast her in anything else if they saw her using such unattractive choices. I told her to use herself and to use humor. She said that the director had told her to do it this way. I replied that the director was obviously inexperienced, so she should present him with another choice and he would see it was better. Her action could be to tell her partner, "I am someone you can't mess around with." "Hey!" should demand attention. "I know what you did" could have a game in it, as if she were having fun saying, "Watch out! I have your number!" The "You creep" does not need to be said with disgust. A better choice for these lines is humorous disbelief that anyone could sink that low. Each choice is believable, but the first one revealed nothing nice about the actress. The second choice showed her humor, intelligence, and strength.

Maggie Smith had a line in Robert Altman's *Gosford Park* in which she puts down a woman who wore the same dinner dress night after night because her luggage had not arrived. The line was, "Green is such a tiresome color." If the line is done as a weak, dismissive, nasty observation, it makes the speaker seem unattractive. Maggie Smith used all her energy to deliver a devastating put-down with (I'm positive) her stomach muscles tightening on *tiresome*. As in "Green (slight pause) is such a *tiresome* color." Her intention was to make other guests laugh, and the audience howled. See anything Maggie Smith does. She's a brilliant example of focused energy and specificity.

Stage Versus Film Acting

Don't think of the two techniques as radically different. They both require the same choices and the same energy. It is wrong to think of acting for film as "natural" and therefore needing less energy or needing to be toned down. Jack Nicholson and Chris Rock both have huge energy in whatever role they have, and we believe them. The biggest difference between stage and film acting is the *adjustment in volume* needed to be heard by a large audience. In film, however, unlike stage acting, the most fleeting expressions are caught by the camera. The camera reads silent dialogue. Stage actors sometimes need to be broader to make themselves heard, but stage actors still need to use themselves and look out of their own eyes. Never weaken your energy or what you are Fighting For because you are in front of a camera. Never play an unbelievable character because you are on stage. Use yourself at all times.

Blocking and your use of props must support what you are fighting for.

Don't use props and blocking to keep busy. Use them to reflect the emotion of the scene and to support your action. If your action is to punish someone for their sloppiness you might say, "Look how much trouble you cause me," as you fling all their mess into a closet.

If your action is to show your partner you are in love and want to have sex, you will handle the props in a sensuous way. For the famous fake orgasm scene in the restaurant in *When Harry Met Sally*, Meg Ryan unconsciously slid her hand up and down a wine glass. The director was delighted and did a close-up of her hand.

My pet peeve, the favorite of amateur stage productions, is salad making. Back and forth the actor goes to the refrigerator, tediously getting the ingredients and chopping up lettuce and cucumbers while carrying on a conversation. If a director forces you to make a salad, then chop up the vegetable with anger, or handle the lettuce sensually. Or bite down on a cherry tomato as though it's the head of your partner.

Blocking should also reflect emotions. Only move when you want to get away from someone or want to move closer. Random movements or frenetic activity are irritating to an audience. Many actors move out of nervousness. Instead they should hold their ground and stand up straight. I tell my students to "keep their power." Shuffling or leaning toward the partner gives up power to the partner.

Another of my pet peeves is the clichéd blocking of one actor standing behind his partner, staring out into the sunset, describing their future. People don't have to stare into each other's eyes, but they do have to check in with each other to see what impact their words have had. They check in to see if they are communicating. Unless it's Shakespeare, people don't muse out loud by themselves. Always talk *to* your partner.

If your partner is saying a line about building a house on a mountain and gestures toward an imaginary mountain, don't look at the fake mountain; look at him. He's making images for you.

Keep the use of blocking and props relevant to the Fighting For. In Los Angeles I saw a play called *The Talking Cure*, by Christopher Hampton. There were three brief scenes between a husband and a wife interspersed with other scenes. The well-known director gave the wife useless props for each scene. In the first scene she gave her husband a glass of water. In the second scene she gave him a cup of tea. In the third scene she was knitting. What did any of the props have to do with the Fighting For of the scene? Nothing. Neither the director nor the actress made the props relate to the emotions of the scene. It would have been better in this case not to use props at all, as they made the scenes stagy and unbelievable.

TIP: *Your handling of the props and your blocking should reflect the emotions of the scene.*

Find at Least Three Ways to Achieve Your Fighting For

Even the strongest choice for your Fighting For can get old if you stick with only one plan. For example, if you are Fighting to get your partner to help more with cleaning the house (and this can be a heated subject going to the core of your relationship), you might plan calm persuasion, which deteriorates into yelling, followed by tears and threats to leave.

If you are Fighting to get your mother to accept your ex-con boyfriend, tell her all the wonderful things about him. If she is not persuaded, assert your independence. After that, put down her mothering skills and then finally burst into tears. (Tears are very effective!)

In life we know when we aren't making our point, and we switch to another tactic. Do this with your acting, too.

I once did a dramatic scene for my teacher, Michael Shurtleff. I ranted and raved and screamed, and real tears streaked down my cheeks. I was so proud of myself. After the scene was over, I waited for him to tell me I was brilliant. But he didn't. "You were all at one level," he said, "and after a while the audience will tune out. You have to have different approaches toward your goal of changing your partner in order to hold the audience's attention."

I should have been sensitive to my partner's reaction, and when my ranting and raving didn't achieve my objective I should have tried other ways to get him to change. I should have tried sulking or reasoning with him or threatening to leave, then given him a calm but effective guilt trip. I could even have tried to seduce him.

I learned a valuable lesson. I hope you learn it too.

Weak Fighting Fors

Actors so often tell me that their Motivation, or what they are Fighting For, is "I want him or her to like me." It's weak. We all want everyone to like us. If your mailman, whom you may see for a minute every few days, acts angry with you, you'll worry all day. "What did I do to *him*?" you'll ask. He'll be a thorn in your side until you can make friends again. We all want to be liked by everyone. It's universal, so it's a weak choice. And it's all about you and doesn't include your wanting to change your *partner*.

If I ask my students what their Fighting For in the scene was, and they start with, "I just want to . . ." I stop them right away. If you say "just," your choice is weak.

Another common weak choice is, "I want to be understood." Of *course* we want to be understood by everyone. Nothing unusual there. Nothing *interesting* there. And it's all about you.

Choose a Fighting For that inspires you to Fight ferociously. Your partner must see your point of view. You have to prevail! He has to do what *you* want.

Summary

Find the strongest Fighting For and *make sure it involves your partner*. Never find your partner uninteresting. The more mesmerized you are by your partner, the more mesmerized we will be with you. Convey as many physical and silent messages as you can. Use your blocking and props to support what you are Fighting For. Be passionate about your goal of changing your partner, and find at least three strategies to accomplish it. Don't play it safe and *just* be polite. RISK!

3 Beats

When actors and directors talk about Beats or Moments, they mean the charged silences when the scene shifts slightly because something important has been done or said.

An experienced actor could say to a novice actor, "I can do more with my silences than you can do with your lines," and it would be true. Beats are the key to engaging an audience. The more Beats you have, the more rapt the audience will be. When you first look at a scene, you should immediately start looking for the silences (Beats). Often actors call this "breaking the scene into Beats." Scenes that are done without pauses are boring.

A strong Beat is when one person in a relationship says for the first time, "I love you."

                         BEN
                        (Beat)
        I love you.

                         JERRY
                        (Beat)
        I love you too.

Another Beat as they both absorb the import of what has been said.

Notice the Beat as Ben *leads up* to saying it. A Beat as Jerry *receives* the words, and another Beat as Jerry decides how to reply. If one person says, "I love you," and the other quickly replies, "I love you too," there is no significance or excitement for them or the audience.

Beats can be created by a touch. A man stroking his finger down the arm of a woman for the first time creates a powerful Beat. Don't forget that all touches must be acknowledged. Actors, especially during auditions, ignore touches, because they haven't planned for their partner to touch them. But touches that are not part of an ongoing relationship are special, and must be acknowledged as special. For example, a foster child rubbed his thumb over my hand in a first and surprising gesture of affection, and it was a significant and loving moment (Beat) for us both.

Beats can be created by a memory. A husband and wife come across the treasured stuffed animal of their dead child and the painful silence (Beat) that follows is powerful.

A Beat can be created by a look. A man gives a woman a sexual stare. She receives that Beat. She holds the look. A message is passed. That Beat is powerful to them and to the audience.

A powerful Beat or Moment occurs after someone is slapped. A silence can be more powerful than words after a violent action. So curb your instinct to say, "You bastard," right away. Take a Beat to give a silent message, and then say your line. The small silence will double the impact of your line.

> **TIP:** *When you have to do a monologue or a long paragraph, look first for the silences (Beats) in the material to break it up.*

Look for less obvious, less shocking, Beats, because the more Beats you have, the more interesting the scene is. Powerful silences or Beats are filled with subtext and silent dialogue.

Mistakes Create Powerful Beats

One day my fiancé's parents and I were sitting on the fence of a riding ring, watching my daughter riding a horse. I was making polite conversation like a good future daughter-in-law when suddenly the horse ran away with my child. I knew she was going to fall off and maybe hurt herself. "Sh—t!" I screamed. Then I turned to the in-laws. "I'm sorry. I'm sorry," I said referring to my language. "F—!" I yelled as I saw her about to fall again. "Sorry!" I apologized again. To observers, the scene was riveting and comedic.

A Mistake can be the kiss exchanged between the housewives, Kitty and Laura, in *The Hours*, or it can be blurting out something to another character that you have kept hidden. For example, suppose that your husband has lost his job and the strain is almost intolerable, but you have tried to be supportive by keeping your feelings inside. Then the two of you get in a fender-bender. You come home and see an unpaid bill and *then* you explode. "All this is your fault," you say. "Why aren't you looking harder for a job?" Your husband is hurt and stunned and too late you clap your hand over your mouth, wishing the words were unsaid. Now you have to deal with the fallout, and that is interesting.

You can make Mistakes without words. Suppose you are a woman on a date with a mobster who could kill you or your family. You pretend to fall for him so you can save your family, but when he tries to kiss you, you're disgusted and jerk away—a dangerous and exciting Mistake.

Mistake Beats provide moments of tension, dramatic pauses, humor. They are electrifying. Look in your scripts for potential Mistakes.

In Tony Kushner's *Millenium Approaches*, there is a scene between Harper and her gay husband, Joe, that is full of Mistake Beats. They are Mormons, and the subject of homosexuality is especially difficult for them. Here is a small excerpt.

```
                    HARPER
Yes, I'm the enemy. That's easy. That
doesn't change. You think you're the only
one who hates sex; I do, I hate it with
you; I do. I dream that you batter away
at me till all my joints come apart, like
war, and I fall into pieces. It's like a
punishment. It was wrong of me to marry
you, I knew you . . . (She stops herself)
It's a sin, and it's killing us both.


                     JOE
I can always tell when you've taken pills
because it makes you red-faced and sweaty
and frankly that's very often why I don't
want to . . .
```

                    HARPER
Because . . .

                    JOE
Well, you aren't pretty. Not like this.

                    HARPER
I have something to ask you.

                    JOE
Then ASK! ASK! What in the hell are
you . . .

                    HARPER
Are you a homo? (pause) Are you? If you
try to walk right now I'll put your dinner
back in the oven and turn it up so high
the whole building will fill with smoke and
everyone in it will asphyxiate. So help me
God I will. Now answer the question.

                    JOE
What if I . . .

                    HARPER
Then tell me please. And we'll see.

                    JOE
No, I'm not. I don't see what difference
it makes. I think we ought to pray. Ask
God for help. Ask him together.

This excerpt is powerful because of Mistakes made by both actors. Read the scene again. You will see that the first Mistake Beat is Harper's when she says, "It was wrong of me to marry you. I knew you . . . (she stops herself)."

Harper almost said, "I knew you were a homosexual." She stopped herself because they haven't gone that far with their discussion of their sex life before. But they both know what she meant. They both gasp, at least metaphorically.

Joe makes the next Mistake when he says, "I can always tell when you've taken pills because it makes you red-faced and sweaty and frankly that's very often why I don't want to . . ." Joe is about to admit that he doesn't want to make love to her. He has never said it before, and he doesn't want to now.

But Harper calls him on his Mistake. Dangerously, she challenges him to complete his sentence. "Because . . ." she says. She wants him to finally admit he is gay. Joe has to take a Beat to understand her challenge and then fix his Mistake by blaming her for not being pretty enough to attract him.

The next Mistake is Joe losing it when he shouts, "Then ASK! ASK! What in the hell are you . . ." Obviously he wants this conversation to go well in order to allay Harper's suspicions, but then he loses it and not only shouts but also swears. There should be a beat as they both register this Mistake. They both know the Mistake comes from getting close to the truth at last.

The final Mistake is Joe saying, "What if I . . ." Here he gets the closest he has ever come to admitting his homosexuality. He stops himself abruptly. Harper knows what he was about to say. She is desperate to have him say it so things can become clear to her. She can't live without having things clear.

Each of these Mistake Beats should feel to the audience as if they were on the edge of Niagara Falls and about to go over. Make the Mistake Beats full and hold them as long as you can. You will have a riveting scene.

Following is a scene with a major funny Mistake. In Larry Hankin's comedy *What Happened to George?* George is married to two women—Doris and Maya. To George's dismay, Maya's children's book was chosen as a winner in Doris' contest, so the two women are about to meet. George is trying to persuade Maya not to go.

                    GEORGE
    It's a small town contest. Miami is South
    Beach — not. Kids —

                    MAYA
    I can't hear you — Lalalalala —

                    GEORGE
    Stop it.

>   MAYA
> I'm not listening to yoooo — Lalalalalala —
> I can't hear you — Lalalalalala —
>
>   GEORGE
> Blow it out your ass, Doris.
>
>   MAYA
> "Doris" again?
>
>   GEORGE
> I meant Maya.
>
>   MAYA
> All right, George, now there's something
> bothering you and I'm scheduling a
> couple's therapy appointment for us for
> tomorrow and every day for the rest of
> the month until we find out what it is.
> Period. May I have my gun back, please?

Of course the Mistake occurs when George calls Maya "Doris." Look at the frustration George feels leading up to the Mistake. She won't listen to him. He tells her to stop it. She still won't listen. His frustration *causes* the Mistake. George's desire to top Maya's lalalala-ing makes him careless for a fatal second. "Blow it out your ass, Doris," should not be said with a dismissive or disgusted low energy. The line should be an attempt to make more noise than Maya. He should shout it at her.

Maya's response to the Mistake is huge. She takes her fingers out of her ears and receives the Mistake beat with seriousness and curiosity. Her shouting is forgotten. It is funny that she heard him perfectly well with her fingers in her ears and the lalala-ing. She takes a Beat to absorb George's Mistake before she says, "Doris, again?"

George should not come back right away with his line, "I meant Maya." His appalled reaction (Beat) is comedic only if he takes time to let it sink in. He tries to think of something to say that will save him, but he can't. Then his weak explanation line, "I meant Maya," is set up to be even funnier.

Maya is intrigued to get to the bottom of the Mistake. She is not angry; she is excited to get to work on it. She is so strong that there is no way George can argue. He *will* go to those therapy sessions. "Period," as Maya says. Poor George. He made a Mistake. Now he's in for it!

Discoveries About Your Partner Create Strong Beats

The following comedic scene from *Widows and Children First* in *Torch Song Trilogy* by Harvey Fierstein illustrates how Beats are created when one character makes Discoveries (or in this case *thinks* she makes Discoveries) about another character. Ma is the mother of Arnold, a gay man, who has taken in a gay foster child. Ma keeps trying to make Arnold straight. She doesn't know that David is a foster child. She thinks he could be Arnold's too-young lover, and she is profoundly shocked. David knows that she has mistaken his identity and enjoys leading her on. The brackets are Harvey Fierstein's.

```
    MA:  So you go to college?
 DAVID:  High school.
    MA:  [her heart!] High school. How nice. [Hopeful]
         Senior year?
 DAVID:  Freshman.
    MA:  That's very sweet. Tell me, David, just how
         old are you?
 DAVID:  Sixteen . . . in two months. [Sees her
         dying.] Something wrong?
    MA:  Not at all. Sixteen . . . in two months
         . . . that's wonderful. You have your
         whole life ahead of you . . . while mine's
         flashing before my eyes.
```

Ma's first Beat is when she hears that David is in high school.

```
    MA:  [her heart!] High school. How nice. [Hopeful]
         Senior year?
```

Her second Beat is after she says "How nice," as she tries to get up the courage to ask, "Senior year?"

The next Beat is after David says "Freshman." Now Ma is sure her son is a child molester.

There is a long Beat as Ma gets herself together before she can say, "That's very sweet."

The next Beat is after Ma hears that David is only fifteen. She takes so long with this Beat that David asks her if something is wrong.

David creates a Beat on purpose to tease Ma.

DAVID: Sixteen . . . in two months. [Sees her
         dying.] Something wrong?

David creates the Beat by stating his age, which kills Ma. Then he adds another Beat by adding ". . . in two months."

The actor playing David must be intelligent enough to know that Ma is coming to a wrong conclusion and he must enjoy leading her astray. His enjoyment adds to the comedy.

This is a short excerpt for so many Beats, but the stakes are huge for Ma. The further the actress goes with her reactions, the funnier it is.

Remember that this is a comedy. The energy is *high* and each Beat/Discovery is more important than the next as Ma incorrectly adds up each piece of information David feeds her.

Make sure that Ma's last line, "You have your whole life ahead of you . . . while mine's flashing before my eyes," ends on an upbeat and is said with a manic energy. *Eyes* should be the highest note. Almost all comedic lines end with an up-tilt. (See Chapter 7.)

Another beautifully written scene full of Beats is in *The Hours*, adapted by David Hare. Laura is unhappy in her marriage because, among other things, she is secretly a lesbian. Kitty, her neighbor, has a problem of her own. Also, a birthday cake Laura made for her husband is on a table.

This section is halfway through the scene. Kitty asks about a book on the table. The comments and directions are David Hare's.

                    KITTY
        Oh. You're reading a book?

                    LAURA
        Yeah.

                    KITTY
        What's this one about?

LAURA

Oh it's about this woman who's incredibly
. . . well, she's a hostess and she's
incredibly confident. And she's going to
give a party. And . . . maybe because
she's confident, everyone thinks she's
fine. But she isn't.

KITTY has picked up the book and now takes a glance
at LAURA. The talk's run out.

LAURA

So.

KITTY

Well.

LAURA

Is something wrong, Kitty?

KITTY gathers herself for a moment.

KITTY

I have to go into the hospital for a
couple of days.

LAURA

Kitty . . .

KITTY

I have some kind of growth in my uterus.
They're going to go in and take a look.

LAURA

When?

KITTY

This afternoon.

LAURA just looks at her not knowing how to respond.

KITTY

I need you to feed the dog.

LAURA

Of course.

There's a moment's silence. KITTY puts her front
door key on the kitchen table.

                    LAURA
    Is that what you came to ask?

KITTY just looks at her not answering.

                    LAURA
    What did the doctor say, exactly?

                    KITTY
    It's probably what the trouble's been.
    About getting pregnant.

KITTY looks at LAURA a moment, unused to confidences.

                    KITTY
    The thing is, I mean, you know, I've been
    really happy with Ray, but well . . . now
    it turns out there was a reason . . . there
    was a reason I couldn't conceive. You're
    lucky, Laura. I don't think you can call
    yourself a woman until you're a mother.

LAURA looks down at her own stomach. KITTY looks away.

                    KITTY
    The joke is: all my life I could do
    everything — I mean, I can do anything —
    really — I never had any trouble — except
    the one thing I wanted.

                    LAURA
    Yes.

                    KITTY
    That's all.

                    LAURA
    Well at least now they'll be able to deal
    with it.

                    KITTY
    That's right. That's what they're doing.

                    LAURA
     That's right.

KITTY is rubbing her thumb against her forefinger,
as at an imaginary stain.

                    KITTY
     I'm not worried. What would be the point
     of worrying?

                    LAURA
     No. It's not in your hands.

                    KITTY
     That's it. It's in the hands of some
     physician I've never met . . .

                    LAURA
     Kitty . . .

                    KITTY
     . . . some surgeon who probably drinks
     even more martinis than Ray, and no doubt
     always takes a six-iron to the green.
     Whatever that may mean.

KITTY is losing it now, fighting to control her
feelings.

                    KITTY
     I mean, of course I'm worried for Ray.

                    LAURA
     Come here.

But in fact is it LAURA who gets up and goes over
to KITTY. She bends down and embraces her. After a
moment KITTY slips her arms around Laura's waist.
The two women hold on to each other. LAURA almost
kneeling to be at Kitty's level. Then, without
planning it, LAURA kisses Kitty's forehead,
lingeringly. KITTY lets her.

                    KITTY
     I'm doing fine. Really.

                    LAURA
    I know you are.

                    KITTY
    If anything, I'm more worried about Ray.
    He's not too good at this stuff.

                    LAURA
    Forget about Ray for a minute. Just
    forget about Ray.

KITTY'S face is against Laura's breasts. She seems
to relax into her. LAURA lifts KITTY'S face and
puts her lips against hers. They both know what
they are doing. They kiss. Letting themselves go
a minute. Then KITTY pulls away.

                    KITTY
    You're sweet.

There is a brief moment, then LAURA turns and her
eyes fall on RITCHIE who is on the floor with his
toys. They had both forgotten him. He has watched
throughout. KITTY stands up.

                    KITTY
    You know the routine right? Half a can in
    the evening, and check the water now and
    then. Ray will feed him in the morning.

KITTY has got up to go.

                    LAURA
    Kitty, you didn't mind?

                    KITTY
    Didn't mind what?

LAURA stands, anxious.

                    LAURA
    Do you want me to drive you?

                    KITTY
    I think I'll feel better if I drive myself.

LAURA
Kitty, it's going to be all right.

KITTY
Of course it is. Bye.

KITTY goes out. LAURA stands in the middle of the
kitchen. She looks down at RITCHIE who is still
looking silently at her.

LAURA
What? What do you want?

It is said just sharply enough to make RITCHIE
turn and go silently to his own room. Then . . .
LAURA picks up the cake, opens a pedal bin with
her foot and slides the cake off the plate cleanly
into the bin. It makes a satisfyingly solid noise
as it lands.

The first Beat comes right at the beginning.

KITTY
Oh. You're reading a book?

LAURA
Yeah.

KITTY
What's this one about?

LAURA
Oh it's about this woman who's incredibly
. . . well, she's a hostess and she's
incredibly confident. And she's going to
give a party. And . . . maybe because
she's confident, everyone thinks she's
fine. But she isn't.

KITTY has picked up the book and now takes a glance
at LAURA. The talk's run out.

The author says the talk runs out. In other words, there is a long silence, a Beat. Why? Because in the subtext Laura has revealed too much about herself—that she is too much like the woman in the book. Maybe Laura says the line, "But she isn't," with tears in her voice that she tries to hide. Neither woman knows how to handle the confidence. During the silence they work to absorb what has been said and think of what to say next.

Laura says, "So," to change the subject.

Then Kitty changes the subject again. She says, "Well," with so much subtext that Laura asks Kitty what is wrong.

The author says that Kitty "gathers herself" to answer. In other words, there is a Beat as Kitty decides the best way to tell Laura the news that she has a medical problem.

The next long Beat is when Laura looks at Kitty, not knowing how to respond to the information about the surgery. Laura should be *working* really hard to come up with exactly the right thing to say.

Kitty rescues her by talking about feeding the dog. They are relieved to talk about something neutral, but when that subject runs out too quickly, there is another Beat as Kitty thinks of how to ask for help. She is Fighting For Laura to feel better or braver. Laura rescues Kitty by saying, "Is that what you came to ask?" Laura hopes that Kitty wanted more from her than just to feed the dog.

Kitty does want more. They hope that their connection will make them feel stronger and happier. There is another Beat as Kitty is too overwhelmed by her feelings to answer. Laura prompts her again. "What did the doctor say, exactly?"

Kitty doesn't find it easy to talk about intimate things. The author says Kitty is "unused to confidences." The following exchange is hard for both of them.

KITTY

The joke is: all my life I could do
everything — I mean, I can do anything —
really — I never had any trouble — except
the one thing I wanted.

LAURA

Yes.

Kitty's lines are jumbled and jerky as she struggles to get out her feelings. She thinks up each word or phrase as she says it. She realizes how inadequate her words are, so she starts over again and again. She wants Laura to be able to empathize with what she is feeling about not being able to conceive. Laura takes a Beat before she says, "Yes." Her "Yes" is filled with the subtext of:

1. Laura really understands what Kitty is saying, and Kitty knows that her deep confidence has been received. Kitty has probably never talked so openly about her failure to have a baby.
2. Laura is also talking about her own problem of not having the one thing she wants—a fulfilling love relationship—which in her case means with a woman.

Kitty ends this exchange with:

> KITTY
> That's all.

Laura's next line starts a new, cheerful exchange, bringing relief from the difficulty of the previous intimate exchange. They speak with optimism as a cover for their real feelings.

> LAURA
> Well at least now they'll be able to deal with it.

> KITTY
> That's right. That's what they're doing.

> LAURA
> That's right.

They continue in this vein until Kitty admits her fears about the surgery.

> KITTY
> . . . some surgeon who probably drinks even more Martinis than Ray, and no doubt always takes a six-iron to the green. Whatever that may mean.

There is a Beat as Kitty struggles to get herself together.

Laura also receives the Beat (Mistake Beat) that Kitty revealed her bitter and negative feelings about her husband without meaning to. Kitty tries to cover her disloyalty by saying:

<pre>
                    KITTY
    I mean, of course I'm worried for Ray.
</pre>

Laura isn't fooled. They have shared so much emotion and revealed so much about themselves that they are comfortable enough now to hug. Laura's sexual feelings overcome her and she kisses Kitty on her forehead "lingeringly," the author says. The actor playing Kitty should not play dumb about what is going on. She knows the hug is sexual.

Kitty says a few more things about Ray to try to normalize the situation, but Laura pays no attention. She kisses Kitty, and Kitty responds.

When Kitty pulls away there is a small Beat, which acknowledges what has happened between them. Then Kitty covers by saying:

<pre>
                    KITTY
    You're sweet.
</pre>

There are several choices for this line. Kitty could say it lovingly after the kiss. Another, and perhaps more interesting choice, is for Kitty to cover up the kiss (her Mistake) and her sexual response as nothing but a light, friendly moment. In every line after the kiss Kitty dismisses the importance of the kiss.

Laura wants to talk about it. She wants it to mean something to Kitty, so her next line is:

<pre>
                    LAURA
    Kitty, you didn't mind?
</pre>

Kitty fixes the Mistake of the kiss by pretending it never happened.

<pre>
                    KITTY
    Didn't mind what?
</pre>

Laura tries to get back to the intimacy they had with:

<pre>
                    LAURA
    Kitty, it's going to be all right.
</pre>

Again Kitty dismisses more intimate talk by saying lightly:

                          KITTY
       Of course it is. Bye.

After Kitty leaves there is a Beat during which Laura's frustrations and
misery overwhelm her. The precious, and in her mind, only chance
of finding a soul mate is lost. She is devastated, so she expresses her
anger by snapping at her son, Ritchie, and dumping her husband's
birthday cake in the trash. They both represent the ties of the straight
world. Laura's blocking and her handling of the props illustrate her
emotions. After she takes action, she can take a Beat to think about
what happened with Kitty.

Beats save a scene from going back and forth on the same level, which
can make an audience's eyes glaze over. Look at the following scene,
which could easily turn into a tedious although heated argument.
The characters, a crazed unemployed woman (Dina) and a secretary
(Sandra) argue back and forth and nothing is resolved. Read it again
and look for the biggest Beat in the scene. Then imagine taking that
Beat further than all the rest. Make a huge event/Beat out of it. Which
is the line?

SANDRA: You have received five checks in the last
          five months.
  DINA: I have not received any checks. I have not
          been employed by this company for ages.
          Your records are wrong.
SANDRA: Ma'am, these checks were cashed. This is
          your signature.
  DINA: No it's not. I don't write like a kid. Look
          at those signatures again. I never received
          these checks. I don't have a job. I don't
          have enough money to support my kids!
SANDRA: Ma'am, the checks were sent to your address
          and they were cashed.
  DINA: I did not receive them. I did not cash
          them. These were cashed by someone else!
SANDRA: Our records show you erroneously received
          five checks after you left our company.

	Therefore you owe our office over fifteen hundred dollars.
DINA:	I owe you? Listen to me. I did not get the checks. I am not employed.
SANDRA:	Ma'am, I am sorry but all I can do is tell you what the records say. You owe a payment to our office.
DINA:	I do not.
SANDRA:	Whoa. Whoa. Whoa. Step away from this desk before I call security.
DINA:	No! I want my checks! I want my money! I want it now! You owe me. I don't owe you.

Let's look at the scene again line by line.

SANDRA:	You have received five checks in the last five months.

> **TIP:** *Start as if you were in the middle of a scene whenever possible. This is true for improvisations, too.*

Sandra should be trying to be pleasant, although the feeling should be that she and Dina are in the middle of the scene and already tempers are rising.

DINA:	I have not received any checks. I have not been employed by this company for ages. Your records are wrong.

We should see Dina working hard to keep her temper. She makes each line very clear to Sandra. She takes time between the lines to think up the next thing. Each one builds in importance.

SANDRA:	Ma'am, these checks were cashed. This is your signature.

Sandra can use the word *Ma'am* to show her patience. Then she sets out the facts—patiently.

DINA:	No it's not. I don't write like a kid. Look at those signatures again. I never received these checks. I don't have a job. I don't have enough money to support my kids!

Risk by going so far as to grab the checks and then throw them down. Both characters can register the Beat of the violence. Her last two lines about not having a job and about her kids are a plea to Sandra.

Dina uses the last line about the kids as another tactic. Remember to always look for more than one way to get what you are Fighting For. If you are playing Dina, you should choose high stakes such as a sick husband, or choose that you are a single Mom and have so little money that you can't even pay what you owe a babysitter. You are desperate.

Don't run Dina's sentences together. She is thinking them up as she says each one. The second one is more important than the first. She can be angrier than ever because Sandra was not sympathetic about her children.

SANDRA: Ma'am, these checks were sent to your
        address and they were cashed.

Sandra takes the Beat to register Dina's grabbing the checks. She can even give a small polite laugh as if she is saying, "You could be right and I hear you but I don't have a choice." Sandra is sympathetic. She sees Dina is desperate. The more sympathetic Sandra is, the more we will like her.

Risk by having Sandra take the time to count the checks to prove her point.

DINA: I did not receive them. I did not cash
      them. These were cashed by someone else!

Each sentence is separated from the one before to make the points stronger. The last sentence shows her barely controlled fury.

SANDRA: Our records show you erroneously received
        five checks after you left our company.
        Therefore you owe our office over fifteen
        hundred dollars.

These sentences should be separated too. If you are playing Sandra, take a Beat before saying *therefore* to gain control. Although the second line could be said with distinct pleasure as Sandra wins this round, don't make Sandra a one-note nasty woman. Give her dimensions of humor, sympathy, exasperation, understanding, and impatience. People are complicated!

> DINA: I owe you? Listen to me. I did not get the checks. I am not employed.

The first sentence is said with total incredulity. Emphasize the *I* and the *you* in "*I* owe *you*? Dina makes the giant Discovery that not only will she get no money; Sandra thinks she owes money, as well. This is huge. Then Dina makes a final effort to calm herself. She wants to be heard. When she says, "Listen to me," she really wants Sandra to hear. Dina says, "I did not get the checks" with control, but then she can make a Mistake Beat and shout the last line, "I am not employed."

> SANDRA: Ma'am, I am sorry but all I can do is tell you what the records say. You owe a payment to our office.

Sandra can get Dina's attention with "Ma'am." She wants Dina to listen. (Beat) Then Sandra sets out the facts for the last time. There can still be that maddening (to Dina) self-satisfaction Sandra has in being right.

Sandra deals with this kind of situation all day and she *knows* she is right. Sandra's part is the hardest because she is a supporting player, so make sure she is never mean or weary, or she will be unsympathetic. She almost always says "Ma'am" before she addresses Dina. Those *Ma'ams* should be specific each time. Sometimes Sandra says them to calm Dina down. Sometimes to show respect. Sometimes because Sandra can't be bothered to remember Dina's name. Each *Ma'am* should have a small Beat in front of it.

> DINA: I do not.

With this line many actors would just say "I do not," as if it were one more line in the argument. But think how far it is possible to go. Make the line a threat. Look at Sandra's next line about calling security. She is scared.

What could Dina do to scare her? Each word can come out separately. *I. Do. Not.* A silent Beat before the line is scary too. Silent and deadly. Danger is exciting.

Dina can become totally enraged and make a huge Mistake. She could go crazy and slam her fist on the desk. She could attempt to reach across the desk and grab the front of Sandra's blouse.

```
SANDRA:   Whoa. Whoa. Whoa. Step away from this desk
          before I call security.
```

Sandra makes a Discovery (Beat) that Dina is dangerous. She takes a (frantic) Beat to decide what to do. Then she threatens to call security.

```
  DINA:   No! I want my checks! I want my money! I
          want it now! You owe me. I don't owe you.
```

By this time Dina has lost it completely. She is raving. We know she will be grabbed by security and put away.

If you approach this scene with these strong Beats, the director will be impressed with your talent. You will make him look good. If you can go this far, the director will know you are experienced and will want to hire you for every project he does.

Summary

Look for Beats throughout your script. They may come from information you give or from information you receive, from gentle touches, sexual advances, or slaps, from Discoveries, or from Mistakes. The more Beats you find or receive, and the more important you make them, the more intense your performance will be. Physicalize your choices with slaps or touches or shoving or even sexual advances to add drama and emphasis to the Beats.

◼4◼ **Subtext**

The first thing we do in my class is a script analysis. I choose challenging scenes, and after I allow about half an hour to work on the
scene, my students read them with all the tools they have learned.
(For most real auditions, you are given at least overnight to prepare.)
Sometimes, to my disappointment, a few of my less experienced students say the words of the scene with meaning and emotion, but they
fail to get much subtext. There is no history. No major events. And the
scenes fall flat.

The subtext of the scene, or what is going on underneath the lines,
gives the scene layers beyond the obvious surface.

Take a scene between a woman and a man who meet on the street.
The woman is accompanied by her teenage child. The talk is all plati-
tudes. "How are you?" "Fine." If you do the dialogue with no subtext, it
will be horrifyingly dull. But if you choose that the couple slept together
the night before and the woman is still married to the teen's father, each
line has a double meaning. "How are you?" becomes "How did you like
last night?" "Fine" becomes "It was amazing and I love you." Not all subtext is as dramatic, but the more you find, the more interesting you are.

To find subtext it is sometimes useful to ask yourself what would
be the ideal outcome of the scene, the happily-ever-after ending or a

fantasy. For example, an older woman interviewing a young man for a job could fall in love with him. She might fantasize that he will disregard her age and recognize that she is his great love. The interview would then have an amusing or even a heartbreaking subtext depending on how it is played.

Deepen your choices. As an example, think about the subject of sex, which can be a metaphor for other human connections. Sex is often considered by men (but not by most women) to be a sport, which does not need emotional involvement. It certainly can be that shallow, but that lack of depth would never be a good actor's choice. Consider the possibility that each time a man goes looking for sex, he is really looking for love. If he doesn't find it, he will be disappointed and hurt, which is why he can't stand to spend the night. He feels sordid because the encounter was so far from his ideal.

Think of each human encounter as having depth and need and importance. Suppose you are a waitress in a restaurant and you are taking the order of a couple acting very lovey-dovey. Don't *just* take the order. Smile at their silliness. Strive to make this occasion extra special for them, or set down the plates extra hard because you are jealous. Don't draw attention to yourself, because the scene is not about you, but do think about the subtext. I can tell the difference between an actor walking through an action superficially, and one who brings his own full and complicated self to even the smallest part.

How can you find more subtext?

1. Risk. Safe and polite is boring. Raise the stakes of every scene. If you are fighting with your boyfriend, secretly know that this is his last chance with you. If you are asking out a girl, make it the first time you have asked out a girl since you became sober, and you are terrified without the courage drinks used to give you.

2. Add extra information. For example, you could add that you just found out you have cancer, or you know the other character has cancer for that matter. Perhaps one actor has a higher status than the other. Perhaps one character doesn't approve of the lifestyle of the other. Don't make these secret choices small. Choose information that will motivate you to work harder, to be more desperate and raise the stakes. Let the history of your relationship with your partner affect you. Subtext should always color your work.

3. Look for the humor and the games.
4. Always ask yourself what the ideal outcome of your scene would be. What is your fantasy? Do you want your partner to fall in love with you, to tell you that you were right all along, to fall on his/her knees and apologize, or to give you a raise?

Using Subtext to Make Your First Line Grab Attention

Your first line must grab the attention of your audience, so make it strong.

First lines are especially important in a casting situation. Casting directors make up their minds about you in *less* than ten seconds. (Don't you make up your mind about the singers on *American Idol* in less than ten seconds too?) You can win audiences and casting directors back after that time, but it's tough.

Your first line must not only win them over; it must also be different from the first lines they've heard from other actors. Casting directors are relieved to know from your first line that you are someone they can count on. "Here is an actor who knows what's what," they will say. "Here is an actor who will make me look good to the director and producers." Don't forget how boring it is watching actors do the same lines over and over. The auditors want to be awakened and entertained. Making a strong choice on your first line wins them over right away.

How do you create a strong first line?

1. Give your first line subtext.
2. Make your first line an action to change your partner.

For example, suppose your first lines are, "Hi! Come in. Sit down." Don't just invite someone to come in and sit down. How boring. How especially boring for casting directors to hear it fifteen times without subtext. Do something with the lines. Make each sentence have its own intention, and allow time between each sentence. You could show your partner you are still angry. "Hi. Come *in*! SIT down!"

OR: Show that you are forgiving your partner. Throw your arms around him/her as you say the lines.

Another choice is to show that you don't trust your partner. "Hi-ee. Come in. Sit down." (Subtext: I don't trust you for a minute, but sit down anyway.) Your Fighting For is to warn your partner that you don't trust him/her.

Never say the first line without a subtext and an action, or the auditors will fall off their chairs in boredom. If you have both subtext and an action, the auditors will be grateful and impressed. Again, don't forget to make each line separate and distinct from the other lines.

Planning our first line is what we do in real life. We plan our first words to a new boss. We plan what to say if we're going to see someone after a fight. We plan the words of a proposal. Conversations never go as planned, and our partner's need is a wild card, but the collision of opposing expectations can be dramatic and interesting. *Don't politely wait for the other actor to start.* Complete your action right away. Bump up against his action.

> **TIP:** *The action of the first line may not have to do with the action of the entire scene.*

Your first line may not necessarily reflect your Fighting For. For example, if you are going to kill a man, your first action may be to set him at ease so he's an easier mark.

If a young girl's first line to a boy is, "Sit over there," she might say it rudely because she is so shy of him, but she really wants to win him over.

If your first line is "Good morning," don't just greet someone. Maybe you could say the line with raised eyebrows and a significant look to put your partner down for being drunk last night and looking like hell this morning. Or the subtext of the "good morning" could be a criticism about what a late riser he is.

If your first line is a question, don't just ask a question; make it an action, too. For example, if you're a butler and your first line to a guest in the house is, "How do you take your tea?" ask with the underlying message of, "I'm warning you not to be one of those fussy guests."

Suppose you're a soldier and you've heard a rumor that your superior officer is going to shoot a prisoner, which is against the Geneva Convention. Your line is, "What is going to happen to him?" Again, don't *just* ask a question. Say your line to challenge the officer and let him know that you are not just an ordinary soldier; you are someone to reckon with. Or show the superior officer that you are not going to let him get away with it. Can you see already how much stronger the line will be?

If you're going to do business for the first time with someone, you may want to make sure he or she knows who's in charge with your first line before you get down to negotiations.

I recently coached an actress whose first line was on the phone to her hairdresser. "No, just a wash and blow dry. Thank you." The rest of the scene was a confrontation with her husband. She threw the first line away as if her husband had interrupted a banal conversation about an appointment. I pointed out that 99 percent of the actresses would make the same boring choice. I gave her a history with the annoying hairdresser who always suggests adding a rinse or color or streaks to her hair. I suggested the actress should be very firm with what she wants, almost irritable, and then end up with a smiling thank-you that puts the hairdresser in her place. Her action with that line was to remind the hairdresser that she doesn't want ever again to have the other options mentioned. Then she turns to her husband to take care of him too!

> **TIP:** *The first line must have an action and be full of subtext. It is never merely a polite lead-up to the rest of the scene.*

Don't *just* be polite, or *just* be inoffensive. (Remember that if you ever say "just" when you are talking about your action—"I am *just* telling him. . . " "I am *just* asking for . . ."—a warning flag is up that your action is not strong enough. "I'm *just* . . ." is never enough.)

> **TIP:** *Memorize the first line of your audition, so you can be stronger.*

Remember: your first line is *always* an action to change your partner in some way, just as your Fighting For is to change your partner, but the intentions of those actions are not necessarily the same.

Using Subtext to Make the Last Line Win the Audition

1. Make sure your last line is even more important than your first line.
2. Make sure your last line is an event.

I recently had two women do a scene for me in which one was urging the other not to adopt a special needs boy. At the end of the scene the woman who wants the child begs her friend to meet him, so the friend will change her mind about the adoption and be supportive. The last few lines were said casually and went something like this.

```
        FRIEND:  Okay.
ADOPTIVE MOTHER:  Okay.  What?
        FRIEND:  Okay.  I'll meet the boy.
```

There was no drama, nor pauses, just a quick and insignificant agreement, after which they turned immediately to the class for comments.

I asked them to make the decision to agree much more important. Now the *okay* was said after a significant pause and careful contemplation (an important Beat). The mother's last line, "Okay. What?" was full of surprise and hope. The friend's "Okay. I'll meet the boy." was given as an important and potentially life-changing gift. The two women stood looking at each other for a minute, absorbing the momentous exchange, and *then* they turned to the class. The difference in impact was astonishing.

Another example of the impact of a last line came in another scene I gave my students. In the scene, a man tells a woman truthfully that he has fallen in love with her after talking to her for half an hour in a bar. The scene was cut off before the real ending, which often happens in auditions. The last lines the students heard were her telling him she was from New York and him saying, "New York? So am I." My student unfortunately did the last lines as if they were unimportant, and the audition trailed off.

I pointed out that the last impression they gave to all of us watching was of people having a dull conversation about where they were from. They needed to raise the stakes by having the man think it is an amazing coincidence that they are from the same place, and a great omen of their successful future. She must see that he takes this coincidence seriously, and for one moment she too thinks the coincidence could be an omen of their future. If they hold that mutual Discovery at the end of the scene, then we have a powerful ending.

Most important, the auditors are left with a final impression of strong actors able to create subtext.

Pain

Often the hidden pain of the character provides subtext.

When I feel that my students are not delving deeply enough into the subtext of a scene, I ask them to look at the neurosis of the character. For example, I coached a student doing a film in which his character, while on drugs, had severely beaten a young man. His work was superficial until I suggested he ask himself why his character had been on drugs. The actor found the reason in his own pain of being an adopted child with cold parents. Once he had accessed his pain and used it to give the character a reason for drug use, the scene became not only believable but heartbreaking.

I coached a Latino actor, a straight man, for the part of a flamboyant gay. He was finding the part difficult until I told him that often gay men make themselves effeminate to give the message to the world, "I'm telling you I'm gay before you can put me down for it." The underlying reason or subtext, is, of course, the pain gays suffer from bigots.

The female character in *Fatal Attraction*, who stalked her married lover and boiled his pet rabbit whole for his family to find on his stove, had immense pain, or she would not have behaved so bizarrely. If you are playing her role, you have to understand what motivates her. Perhaps her childhood was loveless, and when she finds love she grabs on with desperation. Maybe she feels she will die if she loses a relationship. Perhaps her need to punish anyone who doesn't love her has been getting worse through her life. If you play her before the affair goes wrong, her underlying neurosis should slightly color the romance. Even if the lines don't specifically show the neurosis, you could always be the last one to let go of a hug, or your arm could always be possessively around your lover.

Pain can be the subtext of comedy, too. Imagine that in a comedy you had to play the small part of one of a series of nannies being interviewed for a job. Your character is written as nuts and way too eager to please. The parents are appalled, and you don't get hired. If you just fake your part and make it crazy without giving it a base or a reason, you won't be believed. Pick the strongest pain you can find to give a reason for your crazy behavior. Perhaps you let two kids die because you left them in a hot car. You just got out of jail and you want to make up for your crime by being the best nanny in the world. Your pain will give you the over-eager desperation that the parents sense is unhealthy.

Men especially find it hard to reveal pain or hurt because they have been trained not to, but actors have to learn to be open. Vulnerability creates a riveting subtext. Anger is always based in past pain. (Happy, contented people seldom get angry. They let things wash over them. But they are not as intriguing to watch.)

TIP: *If you show anger, ground yourself in the hurt that caused it.*

This segment of a scene from Lanford Wilson's *21 Short Plays* illustrates a comedy that is built on accessing pain. This comedy is called *Abstinence*. Look at the part of Danna.

WINNIE: (Entering.) Martha, who was at — Danna, darling! I so wanted to be there for you tonight but we have this dinner party every year.

DANNA: I hate to burst in on you like this but you've always been so helpful. I have to talk to you alone.

WINNIE: Oh, Martha knows everything.

DANNA: You do? What is a . . . (Whispers. Martha raises her eyebrows, whispers back into Danna's ear.) Well, of course it is. It's absurdly simple if you think about it. Winnie, you've got to help me.

WINNIE: You don't look well at all. How did it go?

DANNA: How did what go?

WINNIE: The meeting. A.A. The first anniversary of your sobriety.

DANNA: Who remembers, it must have been twenty minutes ago. I was a wreck. I qualified. Everyone applauded. I could have ripped their hearts out. I was congratulated. The rich bitch who runs things called me a brick. I've never wanted a drink so badly in my life.

WINNIE: Don't be silly. We're all so proud of you! You've gone an entire year today without a drink.

DANNA: A year? Are you mad? What would be so unusual about that? This is leap year you idiot. Three hundred sixty-six long tedious days. And three hundred sixty-six long hopeless nights. I've read over five hundred books. I've written four. I've knitted some things: a bed cover, wallpaper for the living room. Johnnie Walker Red! Now there's a man with spine. Aren't you going to ask me in?

WINNIE: You're in, darling.

```
   DANNA:  This is your apartment? This well? It's
           pitch in here!
  WINNIE:  Would you like a cup of tea?
   DANNA:  (All hope gone. Musing.) Oh . . . no . . .
           I've been haunted all day by a scene in
           one of the Thin Man movies. Nick is at the
           table when Nora comes in late, and she
           asks him how much he's had to drink; Nick
           says he's had five martinis. And when the
           waiter comes over Nora says, "Would you
           please bring me five martinis?" (Beat.) I
           want to live like that. I want charm in my
           life. I want my alcohol back. I used to
           have a wonderful life. I mean, I didn't
           have friends, but I didn't notice.
  WINNIE:  Why don't you come join us? Just twenty or
           so, they're sitting down to eat. They're
           Liars, I'm afraid, Liars Anonymous, but
           you know how charming they can be.
   DANNA:  Food? How shallow. People I don't know?
           Without a drink? I'll just steady myself
           against the wall here — where is it? —
           and I'll be fine. If Dolly could just
           bring me a . . .
  MARTHA:  Forget it.
```

During their first pass through this scene my students as DANNA didn't go far enough. They read it with emotion but not desperation. Read it again with the idea that Danna is on the edge of a breakdown and is in great emotional pain. She is going to drink again. She needs Winnie to save her, and Winnie . . . is giving a party. What would you do in this situation? You would work frantically to get what you want. You would use joking and game-playing to make it bearable. You would work *not* to fall apart. You must Fight with every tool you have to make Winnie save you.

Look carefully at Danna's lines, "I was a wreck. I qualified. Everyone applauded. I could have ripped their hearts out. I was congratulated. The rich bitch who runs things called me a brick. I've never wanted a drink so badly in my life."

At first my students only described what had happened at the AA meeting without involving Winnie.

If you *just* say the lines to describe the meeting, even if you give it lots of energy and emotion, you will not be interesting, much less riveting. To have the most subtext, you must be desperate. You must be dying. More important, you have to make *Winnie* see and feel how desperate you are, or she will disappear into her party. Don't run all the sentences together so everything sounds alike. Being called a brick must be the most ridiculous insane thing she (the bitch) could say, and the least true. Each phrase is designed to make *Winnie* see in a new way how awful it was. The last line tops them all. And it is the most important: "I've never wanted a drink so badly in my life."

Even though Danna is sober for now, look at how she is behaving, with few inhibitions, as if she were drunk. Use it. Lose your inhibitions and make huge dramatic points. Go far. Then the scene becomes funny. You should get a laugh when she says, "I want my alcohol back. I used to have a wonderful life. I mean (pause), I didn't have friends (pause again), but I didn't notice." Don't end on a down note. Say "I didn't notice" *cheerfully* to show Winnie how great drinking is and to make Winnie give you permission to drink again.

Go far with each line, but try to become bearable to Winnie by using jokes and humor. "Who remembers, it must have been twenty minutes ago" (joke). "I've knitted some things: a bed cover (pause), wallpaper for the living room" (joke). If you create subtext by giving the scene high stakes, then you will get big laughs from your audience *and* they will feel empathy for your pain.

What If There Is Little Subtext?

It is true that some scripts are written so badly, without layers and without history, that they are really a challenge to make interesting.

The following is a dialogue I wrote to illustrate the difficulties of making a scene work if it doesn't have much subtext.

```
            MOTHER
I want you to go to church with me.


           DAUGHTER
I don't believe, and you do. I respect
your beliefs, but they are not mine.
```

                    MOTHER
Just go to church with me.

                    DAUGHTER
Why can't you respect that I don't want
to? It's boring.

                    MOTHER
God will find you one day.

                    DAUGHTER
Okay. I'll be waiting.

                    MOTHER
God does so much for me.

                    DAUGHTER
I am happy for you. But in my view God
allows war and misery and bad U.S.
politics.

                    MOTHER
God is loving.

                    DAUGHTER
Oh Mom. Let's not argue. Let's make a pie
together.

                    MOTHER
Go to church just today.

                    DAUGHTER
One day I will.

A great choice for this dialogue is for the characters to be hugely angry and disappointed at each other for their difference in beliefs. But let me make it harder for you. What if they are part of a family that has been established as getting along well? Your only other choice with a boring script like this (and you will have to do lots of bad material) is to use unexpected humor.

On the daughter's line, "Why can't you respect that I don't want to?" laugh out loud as if you have been over this a hundred times.

On "It's boring," use a game. Stretch out the word *borr-ing*. Let the mother laugh back at her daughter. The mother knows she won't win at this moment, and she can think her daughter is funny. She may even be secretly proud of her daughter's unconventional attitudes. The mother's line "God will find you one day" can be a mock threat.

When the daughter makes the joke about God and U.S. politics, she should laugh out loud at her own joke. Her pleasure in her dumb joke can be infectious to her mother, too.

The line about making a pie can be a phrase the family uses when things become heated, or they can both think it is funny because the daughter is a notoriously bad cook.

The mother shouldn't say any more, and she knows it. But she can't help adding, "Go to church just today." In order not to irritate her daughter, the mother could say the line with teasing tone. It makes us like the mother. We won't be interested in her if she is *just* a stern churchgoer.

The daughter's last line, "One day I will," could be a smiling gift to her mother. Her mother could receive it with a small Beat. The audience should see that their differences are real and important, but they deal with them by game-playing with a loving and fun attitude.

> **TIP:** *Humor can give subtext to the most mundane material.*

Summary

The lesson is not to settle for the surface meaning. Remember, almost anyone can read lines with meaning and a modicum of emotion. You have to do *much* more. You have to make the first and last lines different in subtext and in your Fighting For from the scene. You have to provide subtext for every scene and for individual lines. Ordinary conversation is not fascinating to an audience. Only when you invest scenes with a history and an emotionally charged life under the lines will you keep your audience's attention. Risk. Make the most exciting/painful/dramatic choices. Don't play safe. Look for complications, underlying pain, humor, or motivations that will make your performance soar.

5   Be Specific

I t's agonizing to sit through a children's play, hearing them say the lines in a monotone (unless you are a parent of one of the children; then it's adorable). The opposite of that experience is hearing terrific actors making each line different from the other and giving each line subtext and intent. Often, teachers talk about "going moment to moment." This means that each line and each Beat is freshly thought up and differentiated from every other line. Being specific is giving each moment its due, not rushing, and taking time to let the moments be complete.

Suppose children are asking you for a treat. Your lines are, "Well, I'm not sure. Maybe, if you're good." Instead of making all the lines sound the same, you could play a game. "Well" could be drawn out with a smile. Then you could say "I'm not sure" with an up-tilt on *sure*. "Maybe" could be a tease. "If you're good" could be a gentle warning. You *could* say the lines all the same. You would be believed, but what opportunities for fun, suspense, and for holding the children's attention you would have lost.

Look at these lines. A real estate agent is trying to persuade her friend, Charlie, to move out of his place so she can get a commission.

```
AGENT:   Charlie, move! Really, you're so rich now.
         I mean, you want to stay here?
```

Too many actors would run these lines together so they all sounded alike. But look at the possibilities if you separate the lines with the punctuation marks and make each phrase different from the other.

The name Charlie can be persuasive just by itself. "Char–leeee," the agent can say. *Char–leeee* says "what are you *thinking?*" The word *move* can be said with a lot of spirit to motivate Charlie.

The next phrase between punctuation marks is "Really." Once again, this word can stand by itself. It can sound different. *Char-leeee* was saying "are you crazy?" *Really* can say, "don't be ridiculous." You can draw out the word *Ree-ally*, as in "Come *on.*"

"You're so rich now" is pure flattery. As the agent, you can shake your head in amazement. You may even take a small pause before *rich* and raise your eyebrows significantly to show how impressed you are.

"I mean, you want to stay here?" Look around at his place with disgust at how he's living. Take your time to see all the flaws. You may even laugh slightly and emphasize *here* as if he is living like a bum.

Now you have made your lines specific and it is very likely you have found more in these lines than did the actors who auditioned before you. Use punctuation marks to make yourself stop to see if you can say the next phrase differently from the last one.

> **TIP:** *Every punctuation mark gives you a new opportunity to stop and make the next phrase go in a different direction.*

Here are a few lines to illustrate how using punctuation can help add depth to dialogue.

```
KEVIN:   Well, I painted my apartment. I know it's
         not a big deal, but it's a big deal. It
         changed my life.
```

You could say the first line as if the comma did not exist, but pausing after "well" gives a tiny moment of suspense. Take your time with that *well*. You may not want to admit that painting your apartment changed your life. You may use *well* to laugh at yourself for sounding like a nut. You may use *well* to look around at the apartment. In any case, use the time to emphasize the fact that you know you're going to sound crazy. You can pause after "I know" also and shrug with embarrassment. Then pause again after the first *big deal*. You can play a game with *big deal* by making silly quote marks around it or laughing at yourself. The repeat phrase, "but it's a big deal," should be HUGE. Risk! Make your partner see how amazing it is. Then the final phrase, "It changed my life," can be simple but convincing. Use humor throughout to show your partner that you know you sound crazy.

Lists

There are often lists in speeches. They can be descriptions, or a summary of faults, or a summary of emotions. Whatever they are, make sure each item in the list is differentiated from the other items. Each item in the list should be specific.

No list should flow too easily or we won't hear the individual items.

If you make everything in the list sound the same, we might miss most of the items *in* the list.

Use commas to remind yourself to pause between each item on a list so they don't all run together. For example, in the screenplay *Good Will Hunting* by Matt Damon and Ben Affleck, Will must tell Skylar the names of his fictitious brothers. He has to come up with twelve names on the spur of the moment because Skylar challenges him.

Will has a big task because he doesn't want to *just* come up with a list of names, which is hard to do by itself. (If you play Will you could count the names on your fingers to come up with the right number.) To be believable he has to individualize the brothers slightly. One brother should be the funny one, one the brat, one the cutest, and so on, so they don't all come out sounding the same. The list shouldn't flow too easily. Each brother has to be thought up individually. Even though you know that Will is lying, remember that we all lie well. Make sure you, as Will, do a great job of convincing Skylar.

Here is a comedy with Ezra, who thinks he's had a heart attack and is feeling sorry for himself, telling his brother to take his wife.

```
EZRA:   Okay, go ahead. Call her, date her, marry
        her, have babies. It won't make any
        difference to me. I'll be dead.
```

Okay could be a surrender with your hands up in the air; *go ahead* an encouragement. "Call her, date her, marry her, have babies," should each be thought up freshly, and each one should be more important than the last. The word *babies* could be made different from all the rest, as if having babies is the weirdest and craziest idea Ezra ever heard of. Have the tiniest pause before *babies*, as if he thinks it up just then. The last word, *dead*, has to have an up-tilt or the comedy will be dragged down. "I'll be—*dead!*"

The more each item is differentiated from the other and the more you make each one more important than the last, the more energy you will use and the more exciting you will be to your partner and your audience.

If you watch auditions, you'll find that you often don't hear certain lines no matter how many times or how loudly they are said, because they are run together or are made unimportant. A casting director may not hear a line the whole day until an actor comes in and does the line with humor or some emphasis that makes the casting director take notice. If you make a casting director hear a line or a phrase for the first time, you have scored big points. If you do something different with the word "babies," they will notice!

And More Lists

Most lists come in threes. Look at this example.

> RACHEL
> There's just a couple of rules. First, be
> charming to her Mom. Second, you cannot
> say enough nice things about her eyes.
> The color. The expression. Anything you
> can think of. Third, tell her how smart
> she is. Really lay it on.

The words *first*, *second*, and *third* should all be said with excitement, as if you are setting up a story, as if you were saying to a wide-eyed child, "Once upon a time . . . " There should be a Beat of excitement after the first sentence. Set it up. Then each line of advice is more important than the last. *First* is fun. Enjoy giving the advice. *Second* is more fun, and *third* is the topper. Energy is important, and increasing the importance of each item in the list is one of the ways to get it.

Remember, each item should be thought up separately. Never run them together or we will not hear them.

Most actors have auditioned for commercials. Do you notice that many commercials have lists in threes? You may find yourself describing a face cream as "soft, moisturizing, and gentle." Each word in the list should be specific. Say the word *soft* softly. *Moisturizing* rises above *soft* in importance and pleasure. The word *and* can be broken in two—*a-and*—which makes the final word, *gentle*, sound like the most important word of all. Commercials are written by committees. Therefore each word has cost a lot of money. Don't skip any opportunity to make each word specific. Each item in the list should rise above the other in importance. Use commercials to learn specificity. You should approach your acting work with the same attention to detail.

> **TIP:** *In most commercials and in many scripts, there are three words in a row, such as youthfulness, shininess, and glow. Don't forget to make each word separate; to give each one its own image; and to make each one more important than the last. The last word should be the climax of the three.*

The Trap of . . . the Path!

Actors rehearse scenes over and over for performances and for auditions. They should. Each time actors rehearse, they discover layers of meaning that add subtext, or they find new Beats or humor and they add history to their relationships.

Actors must rehearse so they know how to hit their marks, to keep in the range of the lens, and to repeat their performance exactly take after take.

However, actors can get so wedded to the way they rehearsed that they will not divert from this dreaded "path" no matter what happens. It is too easy to fall into this trap. Only the best actors remain open to the moment, to getting inspiration from something new even as the camera is rolling.

I directed Twink Caplan (often recognized as the teacher in *Clueless*) in a film, *Sweet Tessie and Bags*, by Gerry Daly. In one scene she had to look in a mirror, put on some lipstick, dab it on her cheeks, hold a dress up to herself, and look pleased with her reflection. During one of the takes she noticed that her hair had come unpinned and was sticking up on the top of her head. A lesser actress would have ignored the messy strands because they were not "supposed" to be in the scene. Twink used them. She took the strands in her fingers, made a face at them, and tucked them away. Then she continued with the rest of the action. The contrast between her pleasure in her reflection and her displeasure at the hair temporarily getting in the way of this pleasure was funny. We used that take in the final cut.

You must use your instincts to react to something new the other actor may give you or to something unexpected that happens. On the other hand, you must be able to repeat take after take or performance after performance and look fresh each time. There is a fine line between being open to inspiration and being sloppy and unable to repeat. Only experience will teach you how to tread this fine line.

Add Specificity by Creating Images for Your Partner

A German director, who didn't speak English well, told his actors, "Make it more pictoral, more pictoral!" The director was making a good point. Make pictures for your partner (not for the audience). Make your partner see what you see. Show a thunderstorm by using your hands to make pictures of the churning clouds in the air. Describe how tender a new mother was by softening your voice to imitate her cooing to her baby. Separate each descriptive word in a list to make them each distinctively "pictoral."

There are many ways besides words that we try to get someone to see what we saw. The more accurate and specific your descriptions, the more interesting you will be.

Suppose your line is, "I suggest you eat a light and sensible meal instead of your usual rich, fattening dinner or you'll turn into a bloated pig." To make this speech specific, you might make scales out of your hands for the choices of dinners. Look at one side of the scale to describe the "rich, fattening" meal, and make sure that the two words do not sound the same. "Light and sensible" are on the other side of the scale, and those two words also should be differentiated. *Light* should sound airy. *Sensible* should sound . . . sensible. For the bloated pig phrase you could go so far as to puff out your cheeks or indicate a huge waist. Whatever you choose, make sure your partner sees that bloated pig.

Don't make images for the audience. Do it for your partner. We do it in real life. We work hard to make the people we are talking to see what we are trying to describe.

The Character You Are Playing Must Be as Intelligent as You Are

Two of my students did an improvisation about a female boss and her male employee stuck in an elevator after an office party at which they'd had too many drinks. It started off with hilarious drunken teasing. The Fighting For became clear as the boss began making advances and the unwilling employee dodged the advances while trying not to offend his boss.

The boss began hinting that there might be benefits at work in exchange for sexual favors. The boss talked about the idea as if it were normal and instead of being shocked, the employee accepted it as a normal idea. They discussed it without using their *own* intelligence and their *own* reactions, their *own* disbelief or disgust at the turn the scene had taken. The result was dumbed down and unbelievable.

In real life, if someone makes an unwelcome advance, you know it right away and you deal with it. If someone has just been through a trauma, you get it right away that they are different. Even if someone is just in a bad mood, you *know*. Receive information as quickly in your acting, or you will frustrate the audience.

> **TIP:** *Your character should always "get" information as fast as or faster than the audience.*

Your own individual reactions to events are full of subtext and specificity, so be sure to access your own feelings and don't fall into the trap of "playing a character."

Imagine a scene involving a soldier told by his superior officer to lock someone up who had offended him. The soldier's only lines scattered throughout the scene are, "Yes, sir. Yes, sir. Yes, sir." If you were the soldier and *just* agreed to do what you were asked, you would be monotonous and each "Yes, sir," would sound the same. But if you are an *intelligent* officer and are surprised by the order and are furious about it, then the subtext of each line might be:

1. *I know what you're up to* followed by "Yes sir."
2. Then: *I am going to refuse this order. Uh oh. I can't refuse because the consequences would be too great* followed by a silence filled with rebellious subtext and then, "Yes, sir."
3. Then you could get angry and the subtext could be, *I don't like what you're asking me to do,* followed by the third unwilling "Yes, sir."

Each "Yes, sir" is accompanied with silences and looks that send clear messages to the commanding officer. How much more interesting and intelligent the soldier appears now. How dull and dumb he appears if he is only agreeing to follow orders. The more you differentiate each line and each item within the lines, the more specific and interesting your work will be.

Maybe My Partner Has a Point

To make your work richer, listen to your partner's points and, if only for a moment, allow yourself to be persuaded.

Two of my students did an improvisation in which they each had big news. The wife was thrilled that she had just been offered a job that paid $250,000. The husband had received a call from a doctor confirming the wife's pregnancy.

The wife was Fighting to persuade her husband to let her keep the job and terminate the pregnancy. The husband was Fighting to make her keep the pregnancy and give up the job. Both actors were Fighting hard for what they wanted, but something was missing. They were not believable because they didn't take in each other's good arguments. The wife should have let it affect her that she was pregnant. She should have been much more conflicted. The husband should have been tempted by the money for a few moments too.

If you are arguing with your husband against moving to another state, Fight hard

> **TIP:** *Let the arguments of your partner affect you when they make a great point.*

not to move, but when he says something that makes sense, pause for a Beat to concede his good point. For that Beat you think he may be right, then you say, "Nah, I'm right" and continue Fighting to stay put.

Summary

Use as many ways as you can to make your work more specific. Create images for your partner; differentiate items in lists. Use punctuation to stop yourself and make the next phrase have a different tone. Individualize your phrases. Concede with a Beat that your partner may have a point. If you have to deliver a long paragraph, look for the silences or Beats so you don't rattle on. All these methods make your work more interesting. General work puts audiences to sleep. Specific work grabs their attention.

6 Acting Traps

Additives and Molasses

I often tell my students they are pouring molasses on a scene or I tell them, "I see additives." It means they are adding irritating extras.

Additives

If you're adding additives, you might be emphasizing each line by rising slightly on your toes, or waving your hands, or fake chuckling. One actor I know gives emphasis by jutting out her jaw; another frowns; another opens his eyes wide to make a point. Many actors bend over from the waist to add emphasis.

An amazing number of actors slap their thighs to add emphasis without being aware of it. Some actors shuffle forward to make a point and then shuffle backward once they have made it. Some jiggle their legs. To show fear, inexperienced actors turn into heavy breathers, hyperventilating annoyingly throughout the scene. If a burglar broke into your bedroom at night, do you think you'd let him hear you breathe like a steam engine? No. Fear makes you quiet as a mouse.

Other annoying additives are "I mean" or "Uh." Adding these extra words says that you are not giving your lines momentum. You are pausing because you are not sure of what you want to say and can't say it with conviction. Would you tell a lover for the first time, "I, uh, love you"? No; you'd say it cleanly and concisely. Do the same for all your lines. "Uhs" scattered through your work are sloppy. Some actors use "uh" to appear relaxed and natural. It doesn't work. Anyway, we don't want you relaxed. We want you working hard.

All additives have a common basis: the actors think they themselves are not enough. They use additives to give themselves an extra boost.

You *are* enough!

If your choice is strong, if you are concentrating on changing your partner and you know what you are doing, you don't need extras. They only distract from your performance. Keep your power. Stand up straight. Don't give away your power by leaning forward toward your partner. Don't move unless you are motivated by the emotions of the scene. Drop your hands at your sides (I call it "heavy hands") and work hard to change your partner.

Annoying habits don't make you appealing.

Molasses

I use the word *Molasses* to mean pouring an emotion all over your good work so it colors every part of the scene, giving it a sameness. The ups and downs so essential to every scene are lost. Suppose you're in a hospital room where your husband is dying. Your mother comes in to sit with you and tells you to dress better in the hospital to show respect for your husband. The conversation can get heated, bring up old history, and even generate laughs, but not if the grief about your husband pours Sadness Molasses all over the scene.

If you're doing a scene in which you are drunk, make sure that Drunk Molasses doesn't dull what you are doing. Remember that each moment of your work must be clear and specific. Drunkenness works brilliantly to release your inhibitions, and allows the character to reveal more than when they are sober. (It might be useful to have a few imaginary drinks before you tackle any role). If you are drunk and you have a task to perform, you must work extra hard to sober up. Work especially hard to sober up when you have a big point to make or you want to look sober. Don't be uniformly drunk for the whole scene.

There are many types of Molasses. There is Crying Molasses, where the whole scene is done as you cry and your best work is dulled. Go ahead, burst into tears, but then suck it up. Then maybe something sets off your tears again. Whenever we cry in front of people we strive to get control. We may laugh at ourselves, or hide our tears. We *don't* cry nonstop.

Another common Molasses is the You Are My Superior Molasses. For this one actors are so subservient that they never get to be themselves. They become dull. Even a private in the army can show personality to his superior officer.

There is Almost-in-Tears Molasses. There is I-Am-Having-Such-a-Ball Molasses that everything else in the scene becomes unimportant. There is I-Just-Ran-So-Now-I-Will-Gasp-Throughout-the-Whole-Scene Molasses.

Others are Giggling Molasses, Shy Molasses (I am too shy to make anything happen in the scene), and Nervous Molasses.

Molasses makes your work less specific and more irritating.

Your penalty is not getting the job.

Whining Molasses

I watched recently as an Oscar winner for Best Actress whined her way through her acceptance speech. She was tearful because she was grateful, but she indulged her tears instead of fighting them and her speech sounded all one note. There was an unattractive Whining Molasses over her entire speech. If she had laughed at her own tears, if she had tried to fight the tears, then we would have loved her. Instead we couldn't wait for her to get off-stage.

Whining is conceding strength to the other character. Use your strength. Make attractive choices. If you find yourself whining in the middle of a scene, take a breath and start in a new direction. Whining will not work to change your partner and is never effective as a Fighting For. If you whine you won't be liked by your partner or your audience. It is as simple as that. Sniveling and kowtowing are not appealing.

Game-playing with whining is fun if it doesn't go on for long. For example, if I can't open a screw top on a bottle, I say "Unh Unh," in a whiny voice and hand it to someone nearby to see if they can open it. The whining is a game and is taken as such. If you complain in a whiny voice for a second or two and then laugh at yourself, we will laugh with you.

Sighing Molasses

I cannot emphasize this enough—*sighing is deadly to your work.*

Some actors sigh because they want to relax before the scene starts. Many actors begin auditions with exhaling. The auditors hear the long exhales as actors try to get out their jitters. Actors think sighing relaxes them before they work, but all it does is let all their energy out. *Don't* get out your jitters. Use them to energize you.

Some actors unconsciously sigh at the end of lines because they have lost energy or are not making important choices.

> **TIP:** *Don't EVER sigh AT ANY TIME unless you do it on purpose dramatically as a game.*

Ask someone to watch to see if you ever sigh. It is often unconscious. It means you don't have enough energy and your Fighting For is not passionate enough. It means that you are allowing a temporary lull in your Fighting For.

Reverential Molasses

A *really* bad Molasses is Reverential Molasses, which also can be described as Hushed Molasses and Sad Molasses. With this type you get solemn or holy and talk in a Hushed and Serious voice—for the *whole scene*—and bore us to death. The scene from *The Green Mile* in which the gentle giant, Coffey, and the warden discuss Coffey's last meal before the execution is a great example of the potential trap of Reverential Molasses.

> COFFEY
> Meatloaf be nice. Mashed taters with gravy.
> Okra. Maybe some'a that fine cornbread your
> missus make, if she don' mind.

> PAUL
> What about a preacher? Someone you could
> say a little prayer with?

> COFFEY
> Don't want no preacher. You can say a
> prayer if ya want. I could get kneebound
> wit you, I guess.

> PAUL
> Me?

Coffey gives him a look — please.

                    PAUL
     S'pose I could, if it came to that.

Paul sits, working himself up to it:

                    PAUL
     John, I have to ask you something very
     important now.

                    COFFEY
     I know what you gonna say. You don't have
     to say it.

                    PAUL
     I do. I do have to.
                  (beat)
     John, tell me what you want me to do. You
     want me to take you out of here? Just let
     you run away? See how far you can get?

                    COFFEY
     Why would you do such a foolish thing?

Paul hesitates, emotions swirling, trying to find
the words.

                    PAUL
     On the day of my judgment, when I stand
     before God, and he asks me why did I kill
     one of his true miracles, what am I gonna
     say? That it was my job? My *job*?

                    COFFEY
     You tell God the Father it was a kindness
     you done.
                  (Takes his hand)
     I know your hurtin' and worryin', I can
     feel it on you, but you oughtta quit on it
     now. Because I *want* it over and done. I do.

Coffey hesitates — now he's the one trying to find
the right words, trying to make Paul understand.

                    COFFEY
        I's tired, boss. Tired of bein' on the
        road, lonely as a sparrow in the rain.
        Tired of not having me a buddy to be
        with, or tell me where we's coming from
        or going to, or why. Mostly I'm tired of
        people being ugly to each other. I'm
        tired of all the pain I feel and hear in
        the world ever' day. There's too much of
        it. It's like pieces of glass in my head
        all the time. Can you understand?

By now, Paul is blinking back the tears. Softly.

                    PAUL
        Yes, John. I think I can.

                    BRUTAL
        There must be something we can do for you,
        John. There must be something you want.

Coffey thinks about this long and hard, finally
looks up.

                    COFFEY
        I ain't never seen me a flicker show.

If done incorrectly, this scene could be an unfortunate example of
Sad/Reverential Molasses. Even the most sophisticated actors can get
trapped doing this scene. Actors are tempted to say Coffey's first lines
about his last dinner in a hushed voice because, after all, he is about
to *die*, so they don't have fun thinking up the last meal. But Coffey is
not afraid of death. He's looking forward to Heaven, and he's a childlike man who gets a thrill out of simple pleasures.

                    COFFEY
        Meatloaf be nice. Mashed taters with gravy.
        Okra. Maybe some'a that fine cornbread your
        missus make, if she don' mind.

When Coffey talks about his last meal it should give him great pleasure
and we should enjoy his pleasure. *Each item on the menu is better than
the last one.* Don't forget to enjoy the "mashed taters" but then *add* the

gravy as an afterthought for even more pleasure. Don't say them as if they were one thing.

Okra could be said with satisfaction as if Coffey is remembering a comfort food. Then Coffey thinks up something *really* special, which tops all the other items. "Maybe some'a that fine cornbread your missus make, if she don' mind." "If she don' mind" could be said as if Coffey is worried about overstepping his boundaries and asking for too much.

Use a full voice and energy to think up the menu. Don't have *any* Hushed/Reverential Molasses. This is a terrific meal you're thinking up, and you're going to love every bite. Include Paul in your pleasure and make him taste each item with you.

The next temptation for Reverential Molasses is:

```
                    COFFEY
Don't want no preacher. You can say a
prayer if you want. I could get kneebound
wit you, I guess.
```

These lines should not be said as a downer, as if Coffey doesn't care. The three lines should not sound the same. The first one can have humor, as if a preacher is the last thing Coffey wants. Then Coffey works to find a solution to Paul's wanting him to have someone to pray with. Take a second to make a Discovery about what to do. Coffey can be happy with the idea he comes up with—Paul saying the prayer. The third line can also be a Discovery as Coffey happily realizes *as he says it* that they could pray together and imagines doing it. This is a *positive* solution. There are no negatives to this speech. It is upbeat. Think how happy the auditors or audience will be that they aren't looking at a gloomy actor.

```
                    PAUL
Me? S'pose I could, if it came to that.
```

At first Paul is startled. "Me?" He didn't imagine being asked. Then he stops to think. In the next line Paul gets into the idea. Don't make this line a throwaway downer said in a hushed voice either. It is an interesting and positive idea that Paul accepts with a little wonder.

The last *big* temptation for Hushed and Sadness Molasses combined is Coffey's long speech at the end of the scene, in which he talks about being tired of life. Don't *do* it tired.

                        COFFEY
        I's tired, boss. Tired of bein' on the
        road, lonely as a sparrow in the rain.
        Tired of not having me a buddy to be
        with, or tell me where we's coming from
        or going to, or why. Mostly I'm tired of
        people being ugly to each other. I'm
        tired of all the pain I feel and hear in
        the world ever' day. There's too much of
        it. It's like pieces of glass in my head
        all the time. Can you understand?

As Coffey you are Fighting to convince Paul that it is okay to pull the plug. You are working hard to pile up the evidence for your point of view. The first line, "I's tired, boss," should not be said wearily. It should be said as one fact in the list he is going to use to make his argument. It might be useful to substitute the phrase "I'm in pain, boss," and use the word *pain* instead of *tired* each time you say it to rehearse this speech.

When you say you are tired of not having a buddy, don't say it gloomily. Emphasize the word *buddy*, as if it would be so nice to *have* one. Use energy.

When you talk about the pain in the world and how it feels like glass in your head, make sure the energy is up, as if you can't stand any more active pain, which is driving you crazy—not as if life is so crushing and wearying that you want to sleep forever.

Coffey saying "Can you understand?" should be hopeful. Coffey should care about the answer. He hopes he got through to Paul.

Coffey's last line, "I ain't never seen me a flicker show," should be happy and excited and certainly not down. We should see how much the idea pleases him. He should have a child's delight at the idea of this treat. Paul and Brutal should get pleasure from Coffey's delight.

If you, as Coffey, bore us by being Serious throughout the scene then we'll say, "Go ahead, fry him." If this scene is done without Reverential Molasses, the audience will be devastated about the execution of such a delightful, good, and innocent man.

TIP: *If the actor cries, the audience will feel sympathy. If the actor struggles to hold back the tears, the audience will cry the tears for the actor.*

Don't Consciously "Show" Your Emotions

Expressions and emotions are only a *result* of a strong action. Your Fighting For is like a torpedo heading for your objective, and the emotions trail out behind the torpedo like waves. You have control of the direction of the torpedo but not the waves (emotions) that the torpedo creates.

In life we don't plan emotions; we discover them. How many times have you said, "I can't believe I felt so angry (or sad or happy)." We are constantly surprised by our feelings. Fight ferociously to change your partner, and your emotions will come out naturally.

Never give a thought to your facial expressions. (I don't like most on-camera classes because they make you self-conscious about your physicality.)

If you're fighting with your lover over whether or not to get married, emotions will surface when your objective is frustrated. You may be amused at first as he expresses mock terror, and then you might listen to his point of view with understanding. By the end, if it becomes clear your lover has no intention of getting married, you can express rage, fear, and hatred, which can come out in tears, violence, and shouting. But you will not need to *plan* these reactions. They will be there automatically from the frustration of your action not being satisfied and your increasingly desperate attempts to *make* it happen.

Faking Emotions—Indicating

If you force or fake emotions, we won't believe them. Another word for faking is *indicating*—the actor's biggest no-no. It is showing the audience a forced emotion instead of allowing it to be real. An example of indicating is rubbing your stomach to show hunger. Or, again, breathing heavily to indicate fear. Who does that? If we're hungry, who can tell unless we say it aloud? The only time you can get away with a gesture like rubbing your stomach to show you are hungry is if you are playing a game with your partner. If you do it seriously, you will not be believed.

Indicating is pushing emotion until it's not believable. It comes from not making a strong enough choice or from not going far enough. So, for example, if your partner says, "Stop being hysterical," or "Quit bawling like a baby," and you are *not* being hysterical and you are not feeling at all like bawling like a baby, you have to fake it and you become unbelievable.

Sometimes I "act" angry with my children, but they always see through it and make me laugh. Even they don't believe my forced emotion. Audiences won't believe yours, either.

Sometimes actors fake emotions for the audience. They groan to show the audience they're in pain, or they fake laughs or fake crying for the *audience*. We always see through it. If you are working to change your partner, you won't need to worry about the audience.

The solution, of course, is to care so passionately about what you are Fighting For that you have more than enough emotion for the requirements of the scene.

Summary

If you care about your Fighting For strongly enough, your passionate efforts and the different ways you try to achieve your goals (guilt trips, tears, cajoling, threatening) are enough. You don't need extraneous gestures or expressions or words. Cut out Molasses or Additives. Don't allow one emotion such as sadness or self-pity or shyness to paint an entire scene the same boring color. If you are Fighting hard to change your partner, *you* are enough without extras.

7   **Comedy**

Being funny is hard work. Very hard work. Comedy demands even more energy and risk-taking than drama. Actors with comedic abilities work more, even in dramas, because having humor and an ability to play games and to go further than most actors dare is appealing in itself.

What is funny? The oddities of life. Awkward situations like trying to pass yourself off as a guest when you are a stranger, slipping on a banana peel (but only if the audience sees the fall coming in advance), misunderstandings, wildly overreacting to situations, or reactions to hearing that your mother is at the door when you are in bed with the mailman. All of these situations are out of the ordinary. And most of the situations are deadly serious to the character experiencing the moments that crack up an audience.

There is nothing amusing about eating a restaurant meal unless you fall under the table or realize that your waiter is your future father-in-law, and you are out with another woman. It is the *interruptions to ordinary life* that are comedic.

There is light comedy and dark comedy. Comedy can have a manic energy or it can be understated, even deadpan, but in any case you have to nail the rhythm and have the skills to make the audience fall off their chairs with laughter. Being funny is a gift and a talent not given to all. Through a lucky combination of looks, a natural sense of timing, and attitude, some people are naturally funny. But all actors must learn the skills of comedy.

It is the actor's job to signal the audience within five seconds of the start of any piece whether they are watching a comedy or a drama. What is the difference? In comedy it's often the faster pace, the amount of game-playing, the attitude, a delight in scoring points, and, in a light comedy, a consistent up-tilt at the ends of most comedic lines so the energy is up and not dragged down.

For example, a simple question such as "Are you serious?" might have a comedic emphasis on *serious*. As in "Are you *serious*?" with a raised eyebrow done not to please the audience, but as a game for the partner. This line could be said after a night of hard drinking or when one friend knew the other had had an exciting night with a lover and is now trying to pass off the activities of the night before as if nothing unusual had happened. If you say the line "You are such a drag" with the line going down at the end, then you sound like a drag. If you say the word *drag* with an up-tilt as if you can't believe it, so that *drag* is the highest in inflection, then it turns into a game. Try it.

This up-tilt in the last word of most lines is often the difference between getting a laugh and pulling the scene down. If you have a line with three words in a row, such as "I like butterbeans, olives, and tequilas," and if you say the words all the same with *tequilas* going down at the end, you will not get a laugh. If you end on *tequilas*, as the most important of all three, if it goes slightly up in volume, then the audience will understand that you are playing a game and they will be willing to be amused by such an odd contrast of items.

> **TIP:** *In a light comedy, make sure you have an up-tilt on the last word at the end of most lines.*

Things that make us laugh are not always funny or witty. We laugh in disbelief at someone's political opinion, or we laugh at someone for being dressed strangely. There is also an interesting phenomenon of audiences laughing in the middle of a drama. These laughs can throw actors off but they are really a big compliment. The laughs come from the audience sensing something universal that they can relate to. It is a laugh of recognition. We can also laugh with someone because we are so pleased they are happy. A bad joke can crack us up if everyone else thinks it's funny. We laugh out of nervousness or an acute desire to please. In other words, don't wait for jokes to add laughs to your work. Observe how often people laugh at things that are not funny at all.

> **TIP:** *Great actors give themselves the freedom to laugh in places where lesser actors wouldn't dare.*

Comedy requires making strong choices. For example, suppose you wanted to get a group's attention using three words: "Guys. Guys. Guys." You could just say the words all with the same inflection, and eventually get people's attention. Or you could get a laugh if you say the first two *guys* and then scream the last one at the top of your lungs. When everyone looks at you, shocked, you could calm down instantly and tell them what you were going to say in a reasonable tone. Such immediate contrasts in emotion can be funny.

Although comedy is funny, actors have to take it seriously. A friend of mine, Larry Hankin, a brilliant comedic actor and screenwriter, wrote the following about comedy:

> "Comedy is SERIOUS. Deadly Serious. Steve Martin said that and so do I. The more serious or earnest your character is, the bigger the laugh. One of the components of laughter is surprise. The more surprised the character is at the end, the more the audience laughs. Comedy happens in the mind. So the more you let the audience use themselves to come to the conclusion something's funny, the more the audience will laugh. Check out Buster Keaton. Check out Steve Carell in *The 40-Year-Old Virgin*. They are always deadly serious within the framework of well-written comic situations. Watch Ben Stiller and Robert De Niro play off each other in either of the 'Fokker' movies. The more serious they are, the funnier they are. The first rule of Comedy is: *the comedy is not funny to the fool*. The fool is earnest. The character of the clown has no idea how funny he is—he's too busy being earnest to have much self-awareness."

Take Yourself and the Situation Seriously

The following excerpt from a play called *Almost, Maine*, by John Cariani, is a contest between two socially awkward young men as to which one has had the worst date. The winner gets to decide what they will do that night, although it isn't much of a fight as they both want to go bowling and have some beers. Randy describes taking a girl dancing.

```
RANDY:    . . . And I threw her up and over, and,
          well . . . I threw her . . . over . . .
          over. (Beat.) And she landed on her face.
          (Beat.) And it broke. (Beat.) Had to take
          her to the emergency room. (Beat.)
CHAD:     That's a drive.
RANDY:    Thirty-eight miles.
CHAD:     Yup.
          (Beat.)
RANDY:    (Disgusted) And she cried.
CHAD:     Hate that.
RANDY:    Whole way.
          (Beat.)
          Then had me call her old boyfriend to come
          get her.
CHAD:     Ooh.
RANDY:    He did. Asked me to please leave.
          (Beat.)
          He's as small as she is.
          (They laugh. Beat. Chad laughs.)
RANDY:    What?
CHAD:     That's just — pretty bad.
RANDY:    Yup.
CHAD:     And sad.
RANDY:    Yup.
CHAD:     So . . . I guess you win.
RANDY:    Yup.
```

I gave this scene to my students and it was silly and funny and got a few laughs when they approached it as a fun chat. (Don't forget that "just chatting" is usually deadly boring). The scene was not fall-on-the-floor hilarious until we raised the stakes by adding that Randy is still in terrible pain over the biggest humiliation of his life. The event must be fresh. Chad knows how shamed his friend is, and each word Chad says contains much thought before he says it. He wants to find the perfect words to help Randy with this scarring event.

Chad is Fighting to be Perfect for Randy and to be the best most sympathetic friend. Randy is Fighting For Chad to help him make this event not seem so terrible.

```
RANDY:    . . . And I threw her up and over, and,
          well . . . I threw her . . . over . . .
```

over. (Beat.) And she landed on her face.
(Beat.) And it broke. (Beat.) Had to take
her to the emergency room. (Beat.)

As Randy you need to make this painful and specific. Take a long time with each image. He's not happy revealing this. He looks like a whipped puppy. Take a long time between lines and make each image worse than the last one.

CHAD: That's a drive.

This line is not funny if Chad is *just* saying something helpful or factual. It is only funny if he desperately thinks of something to say that would take away his friend's misery. After all that agonizing thought, Chad can only come up with "That's a drive."

RANDY: Thirty-eight miles.

The subtext of this line is that he went thirty-eight miles with this girl crying by his side. Those thirty-eight miles were *long!*

Again Chad takes his time and works *hard* to think of something brilliant to say, but all he can come up with is:

CHAD: Yup.
        (Beat.)
RANDY: (Disgusted) And she cried.

Remember not to pay much attention to stage directions unless they are crucial to telling the story. If Randy does this line with disgust, then he is not suffering enough. He should think that her crying was horrible for him and really hard to admit. The pain and suffering is real and immediate. The small ex-boyfriend coming to pick her up and telling Randy to leave is the worst thing of all. Even when Randy wins the bet we should still see that he is in pain. Only if the actors take it that seriously will they make this scene as comical as it can be.

Look at this scene from the screenplay *The Amazing Adventures of Roadrash Jones*, by Larry Hankin. A mobster, Moose, is having dinner with his family—three kids ages 9, 11, and 13; his mother, the grandmother of the kids; his brother and sister-in-law; and his wife, Annie. Moose is a thug for hire.

                MOOSE
            (into cell phone)
  . . . Charlie — . . . Charlie — . . .
Hey Charlie: no deals. The money or your
knees: those are your choices. Life is
choices. Don't call here again.

He slams down the cell phone and picks up his fork
and knife.

            MOOSE (cont'd)
Middle of dinner. Fuckin' *nerve* of
some people.

              GRANDMA
Michael?! In front of the children?

               ANNIE
Who was it?

              MOOSE
        (cutting his steak)
Charlie Halla, the meatball I'm supposed
to kneecap Wednesday. "Could we possibly
work something out?" Un-fuckin'-believable.

              GRANDMA
Michael!

             HOWARD
         (his brother)
Hey, Mike calm down okay? The kids.

              MOOSE
Hey, Howie, either mind your own business
or get a job, okay?
         (to his mother)
Sorry Mom.

Of course, the fun of this scene is how the family accepts his job of
kneecapping and killing, but doesn't accept his profanity or his
telling his brother to mind his own business. The more this seems
like an ordinary family, the funnier it is.

    MOOSE is Fighting For the family to sympathize with how dif-
ficult his job is.

```
                    MOOSE
              (into cell phone)
    . . . Charlie — . . . Charlie — . . .
    Hey Charlie: no deals. The money or your
    knees: those are your choices. Life is
    choices. Don't call here again.
```

Moose is already at the end of his conversation with Charlie. Moose tries to get Charlie's attention, but Charlie is desperately Fighting to convince Moose to give him another chance. As Moose you should assume that your phone partner is frantic and not listening. This is frustrating to Moose. Finally Moose overwhelms Charlie with sheer volume. Don't make the "Charlie — . . . Charlie — . . . Hey Charlie" small and placating. Don't make the choice that you are *just* "convincing" him to stop. Go further. Yell at him with the first "Charlie." Go higher in intensity on the second. The final "Hey Charlie" will be so dominating it will cause the hapless Charlie to finally be quiet. Then Moose gets down to business and tells Charlie his options. "Life is choices" should be set out like a banner. It is a statement of the way Moose lives his life. Moose might think it is truly helpful to tell Charlie his philosophy, and Moose really wants him to hear it. Moose may even look around the table to make sure his family has heard his deep idea.

```
He slams down the cell phone and picks up his fork
and knife.

                  MOOSE (cont'd)
    Middle of dinner. Fuckin' nerve of
    some people.
```

Moose can't believe that someone dared to argue with him. It is infuriating, and Moose should go far with this irritation.

```
                  GRANDMA
    Michael?! In front of the children?
```

"Michael?!" should be separated from the second line. It's funny if the audience thinks the "Michael?!" is to reprimand him about talking about the kneecapping, when in fact it is about the swearing. We should see that Moose gets his strength from his grandmother. She should not be played as if she were an average little old lady. She should be formidable.

                              ANNIE
           Who was it?

                              MOOSE
                        (cutting his steak)
           Charlie Halla, the meatball I'm supposed
           to kneecap Wednesday. "Could we possibly
           work something out?" Un-fuckin'-believable.

Don't forget to play a game with the line imitating Charlie: "Could we possibly work something out?" Moose could squeak like Charlie or act terrified. Pause before *possibly*, and play a game on the word to make Charlie seem even more wimpy. Then Moose swears again and digs into his food as if his conversation is normal.

                              HOWARD
                         (his brother)
           Hey, Mike calm down okay? The kids.

                              MOOSE
           Hey, Howie, either mind your own business
           or get a job, okay?

Moose plays another game with Howard by imitating his saying "Hey Mike" with the words "Hey Howie." Moose then wins the little tussle with his brother with one line. But this should be regular sibling rivalry. No one mentions kneecapping.

                         (to his mother)
           Sorry Mom.

He apologizes for telling his brother to mind his own business, not for the violence. The more childlike and respectful he is with his mother, the more we will laugh.

Risking in Comedy

With comedy, the more you risk the funnier you will be. Most of the lines in *Seinfeld* by themselves would not necessarily make you laugh out loud. It is how seriously the actors take the situation that is comedic. Just entering a room is an ordeal for Kramer. He bumps against the door; he staggers and hits his head and falls on the floor and the script just says . . . *enter*. Kramer's accidents never fail to get a laugh.

There was an exchange in Seinfeld in which the character George Costanza had been waiting in a restaurant a very long time for an important call. When the call finally came George missed it because the Chinese maître d' called out the name "Cartwright" instead of "Costanza." When the frustrated George explains what happened, Jerry says something mild about George's name certainly not being Cartwright. For only the next line George goes ballistic and he yells with fury about Jerry's unhelpful comment. Then George sinks back into gloom again. Only a great comedian like Jason Alexander would dare to risk so much with one line. It was surprisingly hilarious. (But not to George, of course).

All the Seinfeld actors knew how to risk. In one scene, the character Elaine has a dreary boyfriend staying with her and she is desperate to get him to leave. They overslept and are about to miss the plane that will take him away. Elaine goes nuts. She's so frantic to get him out of her life that she races crazily around the apartment throwing his clothes into a suitcase and trying to close it with the clothes still hanging out. She even goes so far as to force his feet into his shoes. The further she goes, the harder we laugh. The ability to risk this much takes time to learn, and time to trust that you won't be seen as a fool. Read scenes from sitcoms or film comedies and then watch the scene to see how much further the actors took it than you might have imagined.

> **TIP:** *In comedy you can get laughs even if you have very few lines, by listening as if you* can't believe what you are hearing. *You may only be saying with silent dialogue "Hunh?????" but your expression says,* This is the craziest thing I have ever heard. *Your jaw will drop in amazement. You will get laughs even without lines.*

A Comedic Attitude

In order to do light comedy well you need a *comedic attitude*. It is exquisite timing, a willingness to have fun (even at someone else's expense), a pleasure in scoring points, lightness, easy laughter, an ability to see the humor in situations, and using game-playing. Game-playing is saying lines with an opposite meaning, such as "Wow, you look beautiful" to a woman who just fell into the swimming pool.

Game-playing is also a way to deal with difficult situations. When my teenage son hasn't done his homework or has committed some infraction he says, "Mom, you have such dazzling green eyes." It is game-playing that never fails to make us both laugh.

The following is an example of a script that, if not done with a comedic attitude, could be a tedious fight between two married people who are tired of each other. It is from *Fawlty Towers*, an English series with the hilarious actor John Cleese and his partner, Connie Booth.

Sybil and Basil are married and they run a hotel in England.

```
SYBIL:  You said you'd go.
BASIL:  I didn't say I'd go, I said I might. I've
        got to do the accounts tonight.
SYBIL:  You don't have to do the accounts tonight.
BASIL:  I do.
SYBIL:  It's always the same. Whenever I want to
        go out you've always got some excuse.
BASIL:  It's not an excuse. It's just that
        tonight . . .
SYBIL:  It's not just tonight. It's any night I want
        to go out with any of my friends, anyone at
        all, any other member of the human race.
BASIL:  Yes, well, I wouldn't call the Sherrins
        members of the human race, dear.
SYBIL:  I'm cooped up in this hotel all day long, you
        never take me out, the only bit of life I get
        is when I get away with some of my friends.
BASIL:  Well you must get away more often, dear.
SYBIL:  They all think you're peculiar, you know
        that don't you. They've all said at one time
        or another, how on earth did the two of us
        ever get together. Black magic, my mother
        says. (she stalks off into the office)
BASIL:  Well, she'd know wouldn't she? Her and
        that cat.
```

I gave this scene to my students. I had a friend observing the class that night and I wanted to show off for her. Imagine my embarrassment when this scene did not get one laugh even after my best students had tried it. At its worst it was a nasty battle. At its best it was boring. After doing it over and over again and trying various Fighting Fors, we finally came up with the solution.

Read it again with the following in mind. Sybil and Basil are playing the game of killing each other with kindness. They are fighting to
out-polite each other. Each line is a game.

Look at Sybil's line, "It's always the same. Whenever I want to go
out you've always got some excuse." If she says it meanly, using an
accusatory tone, there is nothing funny about it. But if she says it with
surprise, as if she can't believe it, as if she is making a Discovery that
fascinates her and says it with *no blame whatsoever*, then it is a game
that gets to Basil even more strongly.

Another example is Sybil's fairly straightforward line, "You don't
have to do the accounts tonight." It won't be funny if it is just a fact
or if she is calling Basil a liar. If she says the line with sweetness, it
becomes a game in which Sybil is saying she sees right through Basil's
excuse and completely discounts it (with a smile.)

When Sybil says, "It's not just tonight. It's any night I want to go
out with any of my friends, anyone at all, any other member of the
human race," she must say it with no anger or it won't be funny. After
she says "anyone at all," she has a further thought: "any other member
of the human race." Each thought in the sentence rises in importance
over the others until "any other member of the human race" tops them
all. The word *race* goes up in pitch (up-tilt) to indicate that she is not
a bit angry; she is just musing about how bizarre her husband is.

Now Basil out-polites Sybil with "Yes, well, I wouldn't call the
Sherrins members of the human race, dear." In order to top her little
dig, Basil says it with exquisite politeness, a smile, and he even adds a
"dear" at the end to show her how good-tempered and relaxed *he* is.

They have a few more exchanges and then Sybil makes a big point
as she leaves. "They all think you're peculiar, you know that don't you.
They've all said at one time or another, how on earth did the two of
us ever get together? Black magic, my mother says." If this speech is
said nastily it's not a bit funny, but if it's said with a smile—just Sybil
stating amazing simple facts that she just *has* to tell Basil—then it
works. She ends her lines with what she thinks is the killer. "Black
magic, my mother says." She says it with bemused wonder.

But Basil has the last word. He calls after her. "Well, she'd know
wouldn't she? Her and that cat." But if the last word, *cat*, doesn't rise
in pitch above the others, it won't work. The lines must be said so
lightly and pleasantly that Basil believes he has made a big point, and
in addition has implied that the mother is a witch. They each get
pleasure out of their own cleverness, and we must see their pleasure

TIP: *Never use a nasty accusatory tone throughout a scene, or we won't like you. If the words are nasty, work hard to find a game to play.*

and glee. Basil and Sybil score points off each other, but never lose their cool and never descend to nastiness.

Once the students understood the lightness with which the lines must be said, the scene was hilarious.

My friend ended up impressed by how hard she laughed, and also by the hard work it took to arrive at the solution to making this potentially nasty scene comedic.

Another example of lines transformed by a comedic attitude is from the screenplay *Harley Hanover and The Pursuit of Happiness,* by Jim Macdonald. This is a simple interview line that can be said straight or can make an audience laugh if it is done with a comedic attitude.

```
                  ARTHUR
Okay . . . Mister Hanover, I see that you
seem to lack . . . experience . . . in
just about everything.
```

If Arthur says the line factually or meanly it won't be funny. But if Arthur made a desperate and futile effort to find some redeeming aspect of the résumé it could be hilarious. His first "Okay" can be upbeat: *Let's see what wonderful thing we have here!* Then he slowly discovers there is nothing to be upbeat about. Arthur's lines get slower and slower, as if he is stuck in mud as he continues to try to be positive. Mr. Hanover can laugh shamefacedly too.

Later in the same exchange Arthur asks Harley Hanover what he does have experience in. Harley answers with one word—"Things." Think how funny this could be if Harley really searches in his mind for his experience. He looks around hoping to get inspiration. He works really hard and after a *loooong* time the only idea he comes up with is "Things." Harley should sound hopeful about the answer, not defeated. As if he were saying, "I do have *some* experience that would be useful. Somewhere."

Remember that comedy requires a huge investment in energy and a willingness to go much, much further than might feel "natural." With that in mind, look at the following scene from the light comedy *When Harry Met Sally,* by Nora Ephron, starring Meg Ryan and Billy Crystal.

Harry and Sally made love three weeks ago and Harry promptly left her apartment. They haven't talked since, and now they are meeting for the first time at their friend's wedding. Read the scene and think of the most risky choices you could make. Then read the analysis and see if you thought of going far enough.

```
INT: PUCK BUILDING — WEDDING RECEPTION — AFTERNOON
A band is PLAYING.

Harry approaches Sally.

                    HARRY
   Hi.

                    SALLY
   Hello.

                    HARRY
   Nice ceremony.

                    SALLY
   Beautiful.

Sally is clearly uncomfortable. She's going to behave
like someone who simply is not going to get involved
or even pretend interest in the conversation.

                    HARRY
   Boy the holidays are rough. Every year I
   just try to get from the day before
   Thanksgiving to the day after New Year's.

Sally nods.

                    SALLY
   A lot of suicides.

Harry nods. Sally nods.

A WAITER comes up with a tray of hors d'oeuvres.

                    WAITER
   Would you like a pea pod with shrimp?

                    SALLY
             (with all the warmth she hasn't
              been showing Harry.)
   Thank you.
```

She takes one. Waiter turns the tray to Harry.

                HARRY
No thanks.

The Waiter leaves.

                HARRY
How've you been?

                SALLY
Fine.

A pause.

                HARRY
Are you seeing anybody?

Sally looks at him.

                SALLY
Harry —

                HARRY
What?

                SALLY
           (cutting him off)
I don't want to talk about this.

                HARRY
Why not?

                SALLY
I don't want to talk about it.

Sally turns and walks away. Harry follows.

                HARRY
Why can't we get past this? I mean, are
we gonna carry this thing around forever?

Sally stops, whirls around to face him.

                SALLY
Forever? It just happened.

                HARRY
It happened three weeks ago.

Sally looks at him disbelievingly.

> HARRY (cont'd)
> You know how a year to a person is like seven years to a dog?

> SALLY
> Yes.

Harry throws up his hands as though it's self explanatory.

> SALLY
> Is one of us supposed to be a dog in this situation?

> HARRY
> Yes.

> SALLY
> Who is the dog?

> HARRY
> You are.

> SALLY
> I am? I'm the dog?

> HARRY
> Um hmm.

> SALLY
> I am the dog?

People are starting to notice the intensity of the conversation.

Sally is really furious now. She starts toward the large doors in the background, thinking they can get some privacy there. Once in front of the door, she stands angrily with her hands on her hips, away from the guests.

> SALLY (cont'd)
> I don't see that, Harry. If anybody is the dog, you are the dog. You want to act like what happened didn't mean anything.

                    HARRY
I'm not saying it didn't mean anything. I'm
saying why does it have to mean *everything*?

                    SALLY
Because it does, and you should know that
better than anyone because the minute that
it happened, you walked right out the door.

                    HARRY
I didn't walk out —

                    SALLY
No, sprinted is more like it.

                    HARRY
We both agreed it was a mistake —

                    SALLY
The worst mistake I ever made.

INT: KITCHEN — DAY

They go through one of the doors Sally was heading
for and now they're in the kitchen. Waiters are
barging by with trays, dumping glasses into the
sink, opening champagne, etc. Harry and Sally
shouting now over the DIN.

                    HARRY
What do you want from me?

                    SALLY
I don't want anything from you.

                    HARRY
Fine, fine, but let's just get one thing
straight. I didn't go over there that
night to make love to you. That's not why
I went there. But you looked at me with
those big, weepy eyes. "Don't go home
tonight, Harry. Hold me a little longer,
Harry." What was I supposed to do?

                    SALLY
What are you saying? You took pity on me?

                    HARRY
    No, I . . .

                    SALLY
    Fuck you.

Sally slaps Harry across the face. Then bursts out of
the kitchen with a stunned Harry right behind her.

Just after this scene the groom proposes a toast to Harry and Sally
and all eyes are on them. The groom says, "If Marie or I had found
either of them remotely attractive, we would not be here today."

   This film is a comedy. Of course Harry and Sally end up in love
and live happily ever after.

   The first four lines can get laughs only if the effort to find something to say is staggeringly difficult. Even Harry's first "Hi" must be
said after he thought of many other better things to say. We should
see him searching for this perfect opening. "Hi" should be said opti-
mistically, as if he realized that in this case simple is best.

                    HARRY
    Hi.

                    SALLY
    Hello.

Sally too thinks of the very best way to answer. Her response doesn't
come quickly either. Remember that first lines have actions. Sally's
action is perhaps to punish him. She should show him that she is
blithely indifferent to him. Don't say her line with nastiness but instead with a cheerful up-tilt, as if she couldn't care less.

                    HARRY
    Nice ceremony.

The harder Harry searches for this next line, the funnier it is. Harry
could look around the room for inspiration as to what to say. We
should see his desperation and how miserably uncomfortable he is
and how his body is tense with the effort to come up with something. *Then* we'll laugh out loud.

                    SALLY
    Beautiful.

Sally, too, has to think about her response. She is desperately uncomfortable too but she wants to come up with just the right thing to show him she is furious. What she comes up with is to show him she is totally indifferent to him. She's going to behave like someone who simply is not going to even pretend interest in the conversation.

Once again Harry stands beside her miserably. He is searching for something else to say. He is Fighting to be perfect for her. Take your time as the actor. Sweat. Work hard. The work and the misery are funny in themselves, but you will be even funnier if you are obviously thrilled with what you come up with.

The pace has to be comedic. You have to work to think up the lines *and* keep up the pace.

> HARRY
> Boy the holidays are rough. Every year I
> just try to get from the day before
> Thanksgiving to the day after New Year's.

Don't forget to separate the images of the day before Thanksgiving and the day after New Year's. Don't run them together.

Sally nods.

> SALLY
> A lot of suicides.

This line got a lot of laughs in the film. It won't get laughs unless the actress thinks hard about the message she is giving to Harry. She is saying that a lot of terrible things are happening, and he is one of them.

We must see a Beat that shows Harry receiving her blast of negativity.

Harry nods. Sally nods.

They are tense with all the unspoken words and silent messages.

A WAITER comes up with a tray of hors d'oeuvres.

> WAITER
> Would you like a pea pod with shrimp?

> SALLY
> (with all the warmth she hasn't
> been showing Harry.)
> Thank you.

Her enthusiasm for the pea pod is a message to Harry. She is saying, "I am capable of charm and warmth but you are not worth of any of it."

She takes one. Waiter turns the tray to Harry.

> HARRY
> No thanks.

Harry can indicate with a burst of energy that he can't handle one more thing. Not even a pea pod.

The Waiter leaves.

Once again Harry strains with everything he has to think up a new subject. The harder he works and the longer it takes, the funnier it is, especially when he can only come up with the following banal line:

> HARRY
> How've you been?

> SALLY
> Fine.

Sally can look at him for a second as if to say, "That's all you came up with?" Of course Sally's message is that she couldn't be happier. If she is nasty and if the word has a downward tilt, we are not seeing comedy but a drama. She should say "Fine" airily, as if she is blissful.

A pause.

This is the author's pause and the longer it stretches out, and the more desperate Harry is, the harder the audience will laugh.

> HARRY
> Are you seeing anybody?

Harry *acts* as if he doesn't care at all but all good actors know that Harry is in love.

Sally looks at him.

> SALLY
> Harry —

Sally warns him not to go there.

```
                         HARRY
What?

                         SALLY
                  (cutting him off)
      I don't want to talk about this.

                         HARRY
Why not?
```

Harry's message is, "It's not a big deal. Let's get over it."

```
                         SALLY
      I don't want to talk about it.
```

She says this line twice, and the second time it is even more definite.

```
Sally turns and walks away. Harry follows.

                         HARRY
      Why can't we get past this? I mean, are
      we gonna carry this thing around forever?
```

Harry is desperate to make up. He wants to stop feeling guilty.

```
Sally stops, whirls around to face him.

                         SALLY
      Forever? It just happened.
```

Harry is surprised that Sally acts as though it were yesterday. He should take a Beat before he says:

```
                         HARRY
      It happened three weeks ago.

Sally looks at him disbelievingly.
```

This is a huge Discovery to Sally. She is deeply hurt that Harry dismisses the importance of their encounter. We should see her pain.

```
                         HARRY
      You know how a year to a person is like
      seven years to a dog?

                         SALLY
Yes.
```

```
Harry throws up his hands as though it's self
explanatory.
```

                              SALLY
```
    Is one of us supposed to be a dog in this
    situation?
```

Sally's message is, "Ooh, I better not be the dog."

                              HARRY
```
    Yes.
```

                              SALLY
```
    Who is the dog?
```

                              HARRY
```
    You are.
```

                              SALLY
```
    I am? I'm the dog?
```

Sally makes *huge* Discoveries here. Harry sees her as a *dog*? Her reaction should be scary to Harry. The word *dog* is huge.

                              HARRY
```
    Um hmm.
```

Harry must receive the fact that he might have made a Mistake here. He is getting nervous.

                              SALLY
```
    I am the dog?
```

Sally repeats this because she is so outraged. This question tops the last one in energy and fury. Emphasize the words *I* and *dog*. The word *dog* has an up-tilt.

```
People are starting to notice the intensity of the
conversation.
```

Sally is making the Mistake of forgetting she is around people. This is exciting to an audience.

```
Sally is really furious now. She starts toward the
large doors in the background, thinking they can
```

get some privacy there. Once in front of the door,
she stands angrily with her hands on her hips, away
from the guests.

> SALLY (cont'd)
> I don't see that, Harry. If anybody is
> the dog, you are the dog. You want to act
> like what happened didn't mean anything.

> HARRY
> I'm not saying it didn't mean anything. I'm
> saying why does it have to mean *everything*?

Harry thinks that if he gives in he will topple into a demanding relationship and it scares him.

> SALLY
> Because it does, and you should know that
> better than anyone because the minute that
> it happened, you walked right out the door.

Each of Sally's three lines tops the last one in ferocity and outrage. Sally
is Fighting to force Harry to admit their encounter was important. The
stakes are high, because if she loses the Fight it will mean Harry truly
didn't care and she can't bear that. She is saying that he walked out the
door because he was running from the truth—that he loves her.

Sally should say "You walked right out the door" as if she can't
believe it, which gives the line an up-tilt. The word *door* rises above
all the rest. The more Sally goes crazy, the funnier it is.

> HARRY
> I didn't walk out —

To finish this sentence Harry should try to think of another word for
exactly what he *did* do. (He did walk out.) He is saying, "I didn't walk
out . . . exactly . . ." If he worked hard enough to make it sound better we will laugh at his effort to give walking out a different name.

> SALLY
> No, sprinted is more like it.

Don't forget that in the fury (caused by pain) there is also Sally's
pleasure in her clever line.

>   HARRY
>   We both agreed it was a mistake —

Harry is on the defensive and working hard to save the situation. He is using lots of energy to make this right. To stop Sally from being so angry.

Underneath Sally wants Harry to love her. Harry's saying that their lovemaking was a mistake is so hurtful to Sally that she hurts him right back.

>   SALLY
>   The worst mistake I ever made.

If Sally is scathing and mean and puts Harry down here, the comedy is lost. She wins this exchange by using sarcasm. The sentence should go up at the end (up-tilt) because she knows she is winning. She must say it lightly as if it was a big mistake but it's over and she doesn't care.

INT: KITCHEN — DAY

They go through one of the doors Sally was heading
for and now they're in the kitchen. Waiters are
barging by with trays, dumping glasses into the
sink, opening champagne, etc. Harry and Sally
shouting now over the DIN.

>   HARRY
>   What do you want from me?

Harry follows her like a little puppy dog desperate to make things right.

>   SALLY
>   I don't want anything from you.

The subtext is that Harry is a worm, and she wants nothing further to do with him. But she should still say it lightly. She is punishing him by making him feel unimportant to her.

>   HARRY
>   Fine, fine, but let's just get one thing
>   straight. I didn't go over there that
>   night to make love to you. That's not why

```
I went there. But you looked at me with
those big, weepy eyes. "Don't go home
tonight, Harry. Hold me a little longer,
Harry." What was I supposed to do?
```

```
                    SALLY
What are you saying? You took pity on me?
```

Separate the two lines. Each one rises in intensity and outrage. Work to find the word *pity*. Harry has really done it now.

```
                    HARRY
No, I . . .
```

```
                    SALLY
Fuck you.
```

```
Sally slaps Harry across the face. Then she bursts out
of the kitchen with a stunned Harry right behind her.
```

Sally's outrage is so intense that she makes many Mistakes. She forgets where she is and who is looking at her *and* she uses profanity and physical violence.

Just after this scene the groom proposes a toast to Harry and Sally and all eyes are on them. The groom says, "If Marie or I had found either of them remotely attractive, we would not be here today."

Sally and Harry's heroic efforts to pull themselves together and look pleasant, as all the guests look at them, is hilarious because we know what they have been through.

Jokes

> **TIP:** If you are telling a joke with a punch line, try laughing at your own joke to make it funnier. Your laughter can release the audience to laugh. Try it. It works.

If you are telling a joke, *laugh out loud at your own humor*. Get enormous pleasure out of it. Even if your joke is dumb, your pleasure in it will be funny. Your laughter gives the audience the freedom to laugh. Often audiences won't laugh until the actor telling the joke laughs.

An Example of Comedy Made Funnier
By One Actor Topping the Other

Neil Simon's *The Sunshine Boys* is a great example of topping. Topping is when one actor scores points off the other. The idea is that each line says, "Oh yeah? Well how about *this*!" This scene is between Willie, who lives in a rest home, and his nephew, Ben.

WILLIE: I don't need money. I live alone. I got two nice suits, I don't have a pussycat, I'm very happy.

BEN: You're *not* happy. You're miserable.

WILLIE: *I'm happy*. I just *look* miserable.

BEN: You're dying to go to work again. You call me six times a day in the office. I can't see over my desk for all your messages.

WILLIE: Call me back sometime, you won't get so many messages.

BEN: I call you every day of the week. I'm up here every Wednesday, rain or shine, winter or summer, flu or diphtheria.

WILLIE: What are you, a mailman? You're a nephew. I don't ask you to come. You're my brother's son, you've been very nice to me, I appreciate it, but I've never asked you for anything . . . except for a job. You're a good boy, but a stinking agent.

BEN: I'M A GOOD AGENT! . . . Damn it, don't say that to me, Uncle Willie, I'm a *God damn good agent*!

WILLIE: What are you screaming for?

The italics and capital letters in the preceding dialogue are Neil Simon's. They indicate the rising frustration as each character raises the stakes by topping the other one, until Ben's frustration boils over and he loses it. (Ben makes a Mistake.) They must take pleasure in their wins over each other as if every time they make a point they say, "So *there*!"

The danger of such a screamfest is that it can lose specificity. You must make sure all the images are separate. Look at Ben's speech, "You're dying to go to work again. You call me six times a day in the office. I can't see over my desk for all your messages." Each sentence must be distinct from the others and must create images for Willie. The final straw is heard in the last sentence as Ben shouts the word *desk*: "I can't see over my *desk* . . . for all your messages."

In a topping contest you must register what your partner is saying. If your partner makes a good point, you must feel the zinger land. Then you work harder to overcome that point by making an even better one of your own.

The characters must *enjoy* the topping contest—a lot. They are pleased every time they make a good point. The more they enjoy it, the more the audience will enjoy it.

Part of the fun of the scene is watching Willie enjoy his own jokes. He is pleased with himself.

```
BEN:    I call you every day of the week. I'm up
        here every Wednesday, rain or shine, winter
        or summer, flu or diphtheria.
WILLIE: What are you, a mailman?
```

Willie can laugh heartily at his own joke.

Ben loses it when he gets angry and shouts, "I'M A GOOD AGENT! Damn it, don't say that to me, Uncle Willie, I'm a *God damn good agent!*"

Willie wins the entire exchange by saying mildly, "What are you screaming for?" as if he's not bothered a bit.

This following scene from *Four Weddings and a Funeral*, by Richard Curtis, starring Hugh Grant and Andie McDowell, did not make it into the film. The author says he wrote it as a tribute to *An American Werewolf in London*. Read it while asking yourself how it could be funny instead of merely scary.

```
EXT. COUNTRY LANE. NIGHT.

CUT TO: Charles, standing outside the Land Rover,
in the middle of the road, in the middle of the
night, in the middle of nowhere.

                    SCARLETT
        Be careful.
```

CHARLES

Yes. If I'm found hacked into pieces in seven counties, tell the police it's not suicide.

SCARLETT

All right — absolutely.

As the car drives away — the friends start to shout the chorus of, "Can't Smile Without You."

CUT TO: Charles in a car with a man with a heavy regional accent. Complete contrast of the noisy friends' car to the chilly total silence here.

MAN IN CAR

You from around these parts?

CHARLES

No, I live in London.

MAN IN CAR

O dear.

CHARLES

Have you been to London?

MAN IN CAR

What and get mugged? No, thank you.

CHARLES

Not everyone who goes to London gets mugged you know.

MAN IN CAR

No, I suppose not. There's some as get raped. (pause) Shouldn't be round these roads late at night you know.

CHARLES

Why's that?

MAN IN CAR

Maniacs.

                    CHARLES
Ah. Lots of them about, are there?

                    MAN IN CAR
So they say. That's why the heather grows
so well.

                    CHARLES
How's that?

                    MAN IN CAR
Human blood's a very good fertilizer.

                    CHARLES
                (getting concerned)
Ah.

                    MAN IN CAR
Few years ago, a young man like you
disappeared. Chopped into seven pieces.
They never found any of them.

                    CHARLES
Really? (worried pause) How do you know
about them then?

                    MAN IN CAR
What?

                    CHARLES
Well, if they never found any of them,
how do you know about the seven pieces?

MAN IN CAR turns around and looks at CHARLES very
carefully.

                    CHARLES
I wish I hadn't asked that.

This scene is difficult. My students made this comedic scene gloomy,
and no one got a laugh (except for snickers for the unbelievability of
the Man In Car character) until we worked on raising the stakes. We
decided that Charles was Fighting with a manic energy to keep up his
exquisite English manners and make everything seem normal. Charles

had the crazy idea that if he pretended the situation was normal then it would *be* normal and he wouldn't get axed. The harder he squirmed, the more we laughed.

The actor's trap for the Man In Car is to play "character" instead of making the part come out of his own eyes. First you have to access the Man In Car's pain. He must have been hurt throughout his life to be so untrusting and to want to scare someone so badly. You can also make the choice that he is really going to hurt Charles and that scaring him is a prelude to further pleasurable torture. Play yourself wanting revenge on all men because of how you were hurt in the past. Ground it in the reality of your own pain or you will seem fake and silly.

>   SCARLETT
> Be careful.

>   CHARLES
> Yes. If I'm found hacked into pieces in
> seven counties, tell the police it's not
> suicide.

Of course this line is a setup for the rest of the scene. Charles is not really concerned at all. He's just playing.

>   SCARLETT
> All right — absolutely.

Always start in the middle of a scene if you can. We should have the feeling in the dialogue that follows that the awkward silence has gone on for some time and that Charles is thinking *very* hard to find something to say.

>   MAN IN CAR
> You from around these parts?

>   CHARLES
> No, I live in London.

We can see that Charles, relieved that the man started this conversation at last, is prepared to be his most charming.

>   MAN IN CAR
> O dear.

The Man In Car now thinks about what happened to him in London. Molestation? Rape? Who knows, but you as the actor must know, and it must be bad.

                    CHARLES
        Have you been to London?

Charles must not play dumb. He knows that something happened to the Man In Car in London, but Charles continues to be exquisitely polite. This is not just polite social chitchat. Already Charles knows there is trouble ahead. The actor should use his own intelligence and his own instincts about the danger of the situation right from the beginning.

                    MAN IN CAR
        What and get mugged? No, thank you.

Charles should not start his line right away, as if he's in a casual conversation. He should receive the Beat he has been given. Charles has to overcome this awkward answer. He searches hard for a good response. We should see the effort.

                    CHARLES
        Not everyone who goes to London gets
        mugged you know.

Charles can go so far as to laugh here; a social laugh to cover up the awkwardness.

                    MAN IN CAR
        No, I suppose not. There's some as get
        raped. (pause) Shouldn't be round these
        roads late at night you know.

The longer the Man In Car can stretch the time between all the sentences, the more nervous Charles will become and the funnier we will find the situation. One actor in the class reached his arm out to pat Charles' leg. Charles' reaction of practically jumping out of the car, but trying to hide his moving his leg so as not to give offense, was hilarious. By this time Charles must be jumping out of his skin.

                    CHARLES
        Why's that?

Charles works urgently to keep the conversation going as if it were normal. Again Charles can laugh loudly as if the Man in Car is just kidding—although Charles knows the Man is *not* kidding.

                    MAN IN CAR
          Maniacs.

                    CHARLES
          Ah. Lots of them about, are there?

Charles is completely dismayed now. He hardly knows what to say. His energy is way up.

                    MAN IN CAR
          So they say. That's why the heather grows
          so well.

                    CHARLES
          How's that?

                    MAN IN CAR
          Human blood's a very good fertilizer.

                    CHARLES
               (getting concerned)
          Ah.

The parentheses around "getting concerned" is typical of most stage directions in that it can mislead you. Charles should already be concerned. Hugely concerned.

> **TIP:** *Remember to disregard most stage directions.*

He should be ready to bolt. His voice is probably squeaking by now, even though the word *Ah* is still grounded in his need to make social chitchat.

                    MAN IN CAR
          Few years ago, a young man like you
          disappeared. Chopped into seven pieces.
          They never found any of them.

Again, the more time the Man in Car lets lapse between each line, the more Charles will suffer and the more we will laugh. We could see Charles looking out the window of the car for a house to run to for help. He could look over at the Man in Car and then quickly away again. Charles must be planning escape. The actor who was most successful as Charles in the scene laughed wildly after every line of the Man in the Car, but he also looked as if he were about to cry.

> CHARLES
> Really? (worried pause) How do you know
> about them then?

> MAN IN CAR
> What?

Remember that you never say "What?" as if you can't hear. What a dull choice, and no writer would write such a vacuous line. So what does "What" mean here? The Man in Car could be challenging Charles to follow through on the dangerous thought that he might be with a killer. The Man in the Car could get pleasure in that. "What?" could be a game. You make your own choice. The only one that is not good is that he didn't hear Charles.

> CHARLES
> Well, if they never found any of them,
> how do you know about the seven pieces?

MAN IN CAR turns around and looks at CHARLES very carefully.

Man In Car is giving Charles a specific message: *I know about the seven pieces because I am the one who cut them up.*

> CHARLES
> I wish I hadn't asked that.

The actor in my class who was the most successful with the last line didn't say it in an obvious, small, scared way. He made the terrible Discovery that the Man In Car was telling him that he was the killer. The actor, as Charles, made a game out of his fear. His ridiculous effort to continue to be social while still feeling the terrible fear was hilarious. The actor had decided that if he could keep things on a social, polite level he would be all right. So he kept laughing as if the Man In Car was kidding, but the laughter was on the verge of hysteria.

Broad comedy is only funny if actors risk by going much further than might feel comfortable. They must raise the stakes to the highest level and have a comedic attitude.

Rockheads, a screenplay by Gerry Daly, provides an example of a scene that will *only* be funny if the actors risk. Mr. Moffet is a mob boss. His son, Walter, and Walter's girlfriend, Ava, lost millions of dollars during a drug deal when a suitcase full of money fell out of a window and was stolen by a homeless woman. The police confiscated all the cocaine. Now Walter and Ava are explaining it to his dad.

INT — MR. MOFFET'S LIVING ROOM — DAY

MR. MOFFET is in his late sixties. He's sitting on the sofa. His body is small and frail. A WHEEZING noise comes from him whenever he inhales.

AVA and WALTER are with him. They're wearing new outfits.

                    MR. MOFFET
     He . . . fell . . . out my office window?

                    AVA
     Your son pushed him, Mr. Moffet.

Mr. Moffet GASPS for air.

                    WALTER
     Ava, please.
               (beat)
     Papa, Sonny Corino refused to buy your coke.
     Said it was crap. I stepped on it a little.

                    AVA
     A lot. Too much.

                    WALTER
     Ava, please.
               (to Ava)
     Thank you.
               (to Mr. Moffet)
     Papa, Sonny Corino needed a little
     convincing. I shoved him. I thought it
     was the fire escape window.

                    MR. MOFFET
Well . . . nobody will know . . . He
could have fallen off the roof.

                    AVA
He fell on top of your brand new car.

Mr. Moffet starts choking.

                    WALTER
Ava, stop. You're not helping.

Ava fusses over Mr. Moffet. Mr. Moffet smiles as he
looks at Ava's ample bosom.

                    AVA
Walter, your Dad needs to know everything.
      (she brushes against Mr. Moffet)
You want to know everything, don't you,
Mr. Moffet?

Mr. Moffet nods his trembling head. His hand shakes
when she hands him a glass of water. He spills
water on his lap.

She uses a cloth to wipe up the water. Mr. Moffet
smiles.

                    AVA
A homeless woman ran off with Sonny's money.

Mr. Moffet COUGHS and SPITS up the water he's
drinking.

                    WALTER
Are you trying to kill him?

                    AVA
            (under her breath)
Duh!

                    WALTER
Don't worry, papa. I'll find the money
even if I have to break the legs of every
homeless man woman and child.

Mr. Moffet's eyes bulge as he WHEEZES, GASPS, GAGS and COUGHS. He holds his frail little hand over his heart.

                    AVA
     That's a wee bit ugly, Walter. Your
     dad doesn't need that on his conscience
     since he's going to meet Saint Peter
     real soon.

A weird noise comes from Mr. Moffet.

                    AVA
     He needs to know how you left all his
     cocaine in the office.
                    (Mr. Moffet MOANS)
     On top of your desk . . .
                    (Mr. Moffet GROANS)
     Millions of dollars worth of cocaine. I'm
     sure the police are having a snorting
     good time.

Mr. Moffet has spasmodic convulsions.

The producers asked me to direct some scenes from this script to make a film short to interest investors. The scene was difficult to make comedic, but when we succeeded the crew was cracking up silently as the actors did the first master. When actors get the crew to laugh they have received a high compliment.

The secret to making it funny was for the actors to risk by making the stakes huge. Ava's Fighting For was to kill weak Mr. Moffet to get the rest of his money. She thinks she can do it by shocking him to death. But to make us laugh we have to see her huge *enjoyment* of the process. Ava practically danced with glee as she thought up new ways to provoke Mr. Moffet into a stroke or a heart attack.

Mr. Moffet got huge laughs when he coughed and wheezed and sputtered as he reacted to terrible news. The further he went with almost dying of emotion the more laughs he got. He was not content to just cough politely. His body convulsed. He grabbed his throat. He wheezed as though each breath were his last. Occasionally, he grabbed his oxygen. When he got some particularly bad news, he grabbed his oxygen and jammed it in his mouth.

Walter Fought to keep the situation steady in spite of his girl-friend's bizarre behavior. His earnestness and attempts to please his father and to make excuses for himself were comedic.

<pre>
                    MR. MOFFET
    He . . . fell . . . out my office window?
</pre>

The pauses are good ways to emphasize Mr. Moffet's incredulity. He can hardly get the words out, he is so appalled. Do you see that the scene is starting in the middle? It is always good to start a scene as if it has been going on for a while. It adds history and subtext.

<pre>
                    AVA
    Your son pushed him, Mr. Moffet.
</pre>

Ava takes huge pleasure in tattling on Walter. She must enjoy stirring things up. She should emphasize the word *pushed*.

<pre>
Mr. Moffet GASPS for air.
</pre>

<pre>
                    WALTER
    Ava, please.
</pre>

Don't forget that Walter is a mobster's son. He will not take a woman's misbehavior lightly. He can grab Ava's arm or shove her slightly. Then she can be furious and go even further. As Walter, don't be polite here. But remember that Ava is stunning and Walter doesn't want to lose her, so he is conflicted.

<pre>
                    (beat)
                WALTER (cont)
    Papa, Sonny Corino refused to buy your coke.
    Said it was crap. I stepped on it a little.
</pre>

Walter has respect for his powerful father. He has messed up spectacularly. He is Fighting to get back his father's trust. The three sentences are separate thoughts. The first one, that Sonny has refused to buy the coke, is momentous. Choose that Sonny Corino has always bought the coke before, and choose that Sonny Corino is their most important customer.

Walter is delivering a big event Beat. Mr. Moffet instantly realizes that this news is huge. His reaction is big. He gasps and chokes after receiving each line. By making these strong choices you raise the stakes.

The second sentence, "Said it was crap," is huge too. Choose that never in this mob family's history has anyone put down the purity of their product. They may be mobsters, but they have their standards and their pride.

Now Walter has to admit that he adulterated the coke. "I stepped on it a little."

He should work hard to make this seem like a little thing. Shrug his shoulders. Dismiss the fact that he has ruined the reputation of his family. The harder he works to make adulterating the coke seem like nothing, the harder we will laugh.

                              AVA
        A lot. Too much.

Again Ava almost laughs out loud from the pleasure of telling Mr. Moffet that Walter messed up so badly. She hopes that hearing the news will kill Mr. Moffet. She is having a ball.

                           WALTER
        Ava, please. (to Ava) Thank you.

Walter corrects Ava harshly. Then through clenched teeth he says "Thank you."

                        (to Mr. Moffet)
        Papa, Sonny Corino needed a little
        convincing. I shoved him. I thought it
        was the fire escape window.

Each punctuation mark can help you differentiate one phrase from another. "Papa" can be buttering him up with a plea for sympathy. It is not just a form of address. Again, the three following sentences are separated. "Sonny Corino needed a little" (Walter has to think up a way to put it nicely) ". . . convincing." "I shoved him" can be said with a mild shrug to minimize the brutal fight that took place. The third line, "I thought it was the fire escape window," is an excuse and rises in pitch above the others.

                         MR. MOFFET
        Well . . . nobody will know . . . He
        could have fallen off the roof.

Mr. Moffet takes charge. "Well . . ." is followed by Mr. Moffet thinking up the best way to deal with the situation. Then he comes up with a cheerful excuse: "He could have fallen off the roof."

```
                    AVA
     He fell on top of your brand new car.
```

Again Ava doesn't hold back her glee and can be literally dancing with pleasure. Her line tops Mr. Moffet's.

Mr. Moffet chokes. He LOVES that car. Make his car custom made in Europe. It took months to be completed. It has ostrich leather seats and a special gold hood ornament. You make up the details, but make sure it is not an ordinary car.

```
                   WALTER
     Ava, stop. You're not helping.

Ava fusses over Mr. Moffet.
```

That stage direction is what the script said. What we shot were Ava's breasts in extreme close-up coming toward Mr. Moffet's ecstatic eyes. Ava has thought up another way to kill Mr. Moffet—she is going to excite him to death.

"Mr. Moffet smiles as he looks at Ava's ample bosom" were the directions in the script.

But in our film he didn't just smile, he hyperventilated and gasped with pleasure. Never be limited by stage directions. Risk!

```
                    AVA
     Walter, your Dad needs to know everything.
          (she brushes up against Mr. Moffet)
     You want to know everything, don't you,
     Mr. Moffet?
```

Ava is seducing Mr. Moffet and she throws a look at Walter to make sure he is getting jealous. Ava is having a ball. She loves the attention. Mr. Moffet loves her.

```
Mr. Moffet nods his trembling head. His hand shakes
when she hands him a glass of water. He spills
water on his lap.
```

She uses a cloth to wipe up the water. Mr. Moffet
smiles.

Again, the stage directions were from the script. And again in our
film we went further. Ava brushed the water off Mr. Moffet's lap with
explicit sexual intent. Mr. Moffet went crazy with desire.

                    AVA
    A homeless woman ran off with Sonny's money.

Ava hopes that the excitement of Mr. Moffet's reaction to her touch
added to more bad news—the worst, that the money is gone—will
kill Mr. Moffet.

Mr. Moffet COUGHS and SPITS up the water he's
drinking.

We added Mr. Moffet spewing his drink across the room. It was satisfyingly visual and got a laugh.

                    WALTER
    Are you trying to kill him?

Walter is angry until Ava gives him something to think about.

                    AVA
                (under her breath)
        Duh!

Ava gives Walter a message that he likes. Pick that the father has been
brutal, tough, and unloving. Walter immediately gets Ava's plan. He
takes a minute to receive the news and decide what to do with it.
Then he becomes Ava's accomplice.

                    WALTER
    Don't worry, papa. I'll find the money
    even if I have to break the legs of every
    homeless man woman and child.

Walter creates images he knows will distress his secretive, mobster
father.

Mr. Moffet's eyes bulge as he WHEEZES, GASPS, GAGS and COUGHS. He holds his frail little hand over his heart.

                    AVA
     That's a wee bit ugly, Walter. Your dad
     doesn't need that on his conscience since
     he's going to meet Saint Peter real soon.

Ava laughs at her own cleverness. She adds more and more bits of news, which land like blows. She tells Mr. Moffet he is going to die soon.

A weird noise comes from Mr. Moffet.

                    AVA
     He needs to know how you left all his
     cocaine in the office.
                (Mr. Moffet MOANS)
     On top of your desk . . .
                (Mr. Moffet GROANS)
     Millions of dollars worth of cocaine. I'm
     sure the police are having a snorting
     good time.

Each of Ava's sentences tops the last one and each has specific images for Mr. Moffet. We have to see each piece of information land. Each piece of information rises in importance above the others. If you are playing Mr. Moffet, don't just wheeze and gasp throughout. Mr. Moffet listens to each piece of information and his wheezing and gasping reflects his having heard each one.

On Ava's last line she makes a joke. Our actress was bent double with mirth and pleasure at her own wit.

Mr. Moffet has spasmodic convulsions. Walter is working hard to stay on top of the situation. The scene fades on them all using maximum energy to achieve their goals.

Do you see that risking and raising the stakes were needed to make this scene successful?

Another scene that requires risking is from a screenplay we used earlier, *What Happened to George?* by Larry Hankin. You may remember that George is married to two women, each of whom he sees for two

weeks out of the month. Neither woman knows about the other one.
George is leaving on a trip. He has just called Doris by the nickname
of his other wife.

In my class the first two actors to tackle this scene read it as an
argument only, and we didn't crack a smile. But when it was read by
students who knew about topping and raising the stakes and taking
pleasure in wins, the scene got huge laughs.

                    DORIS
Who's Moe?

                    GEORGE
What? Who?

                    DORIS
You just called me, "Moe."

                    GEORGE
No I didn't.

                    DORIS
Of course you did.

                    GEORGE
No way.

                    DORIS
Way. Who's Moe, George?

                    GEORGE
I don't know. Nobody.

                    DORIS
If Moe's nobody, then I'm Britney Spears.
Am I Britney Spears, George?

The suitcase is neatly packed. He zips it up.

                    GEORGE
It's a cartoon: "Moe the Schmoe" — how
the hell should I know who it is? It's
not important: let's focus on the loss of
$5,000,000. How can we — !

```
                          DORIS
         "Cartoon" is your last word on the subject?

                          GEORGE
         On what subject?

                          DORIS
         Moe.

                          GEORGE
         Yes.

                          DORIS
         Okay. Here's mine: "Separation."
```

You will notice that the first line of this scene is a question.

```
                          DORIS
         Who's Moe?
```

Remember that actors should never merely ask a question. The question always has to have subtext. With this first line the actress has to immediately get that her husband might have been unfaithful. After all, we only "slip" with a name that we use frequently. The subtext of the line contains not only her suspicion but is also colored by her *pain* in realizing that he may be cheating. She is a strong woman, and the audience and George know he is in big trouble. She is Fighting to make him confess. The more formidable my students were as Doris with that first line, the more fun the class had.

```
                          GEORGE
         What? Who?
```

Again, a question is never just a question. George is fully aware of the seriousness of his calling Doris by the wrong name. This is a broad comedy, so if George *only* acts innocent and *only* asks a question, we will not laugh. He must Fight to jolly Doris out of thinking he has another woman, so he acts innocent and laughs *out loud*, as if Doris must be out of her mind.

```
                          DORIS
         You just called me, "Moe."
```

Doris is not fooled for one moment.

                    GEORGE
     No I didn't.

Because this is a comedy George has to have a comedic attitude. He laughs at Doris again. *Of course not, honey,* he is saying. *Are you nutty? Hah hah!*

                    DORIS
     Of course you did.

Doris is again fierce. And her fierceness is in comedic contrast to George's comedic innocence.

                    GEORGE
     No way.

Remember that George is Fighting to jolly her out of her suspicions. He keeps laughingly dismissing her suspicions.

                    DORIS
     Way. Who's Moe, George?

Doris' line "Way" is scary. George is in *ve-ry* big trouble. She can ask, "Who's Moe, George?" with deceptive sweetness. Play a game emphasizing the juxtaposition of the two names, Moe and George.

                    GEORGE
     I don't know. Nobody.

George can toss up his hands and laugh out loud as if he has *no* idea what she is talking about. Separate the two lines. Or he can pretend to innocently think about the question.

                    DORIS
     If Moe's nobody, then I'm Britney Spears.
     Am I Britney Spears, George?

The question should be angry and scary and should *demand an answer.* Then it's funny.

     The suitcase is neatly packed. He zips it up.

We see George desperately thinking. His eyes dart around looking for something to save him. Then with *delight* he discovers an idea!

> GEORGE
> It's a cartoon: "Moe the Schmoe" — how the hell should I know who it is? It's not important: let's focus on the loss of $5,000,000. How can we — !

George now feels he is off the hook. He came up with a great excuse for his slip and he changes the subject. He's in control again! What a relief.

> DORIS
> "Cartoon" is your last word on the subject?

The word *cartoon* should drip venom. Doris is very, very dangerous.

> GEORGE
> On what subject?

The more innocent and casual George acts, the funnier he is.

> DORIS
> Moe.

Doris is not fooled by George's pretending not to know what she is talking about.

> GEORGE
> Yes.

George knows he is caught. His "yes" could come out hopefully or he could ask it as a question. He is saying that indeed "cartoon" *is* his last word on the subject. Whatever choice it is, he has to take time before he says it, and he has to be full of energy even though he has lost.

> DORIS
> Okay. Here's mine: "Separation."

There are three distinct lines here. "Okay" can be said extra slowly to draw out the terror for George. "Here's mine" is said separately, and perhaps she can again be deceptively sweet. There is a significant pause before she says "Separation." You can say "Separation" as a game with each syllable separated from the others as if she were talking to an idiot.

George should try desperately to find an excuse. His mouth can open and close. But he can't think of a thing to say.

Doris wins.

Don't forget that in comedies the pace is quick. Doris should delight in winning and be thrilled about her triumph over the hapless George. When my students did the scene with all these elements, we were on the floor laughing.

Make a comedic choice about what you are fighting for.

The following scene from the screenplay *The Amazing Adventures of Roadrash Jones*, by Larry Hankin, illustrates how important your Fighting For is in making your scene comedic.

Charlie and Janet, a married couple, are hiding in the bushes. They are pursuing an old man who has escaped from a hospital. He is the key to Charlie's money worries. Charlie owes Moose money, and Moose has threatened to break Charlie's legs if he doesn't pay up. The old man, Emmett, has a lot of money if only Charlie can find him and get power of attorney so he can control the money. To understand this scene, you also need to know that Charlie and Janet's Lexus has been stolen.

> CHARLIE
> (to sky)
> Help me. This is a perfect time. Right now.

> JANET
> (whispers)
> Charlie, c'mere.

> CHARLIE
> What?

> JANET
> (whispers)
> SHSH! Look.

She stands looking around the bend in the road, pointing off —

JANET'S POV: A cabin about 100 yards off: parked between the porch and an old BMW is a BLACK LEXUS WITH A CRACKED REAR WINDOW.

Janet and Charlie take cover in the bushes.

                    CHARLIE
   Holy — !
                (looks to sky)
   Thank you. See? Was that so hard?

                    JANET
                (whispering)
   But no Emmett. And I don't see any
   motorcycle either. Let's go.

                    CHARLIE
                (whispering)
   What about our Lexus?

                    JANET
   We've got full coverage. They'll give us
   another one.

                    CHARLIE
   That's not the point.

                    JANET
   Honey, we've got to find Emmett, remember?
   Remember Moose? Remember your knees?
   We're doing this for a reason, right,
   Charlie? Aren't we?

                    CHARLIE
                (whispering)
   Jan, you're getting hysterical. We catch
   Emmett faster and easier with the Lexus.

                    JANET
                (whispering)
   Honey, this guy is nuts. He's got a loaded
   gun and he's willing to use it. Charlie,

```
it's  not  supposed  to  be  like  this.  I  want
a  family.  I  want  a  home.  I  want  my  Mom  to
come  visit  us  and  the  kids.
```

                    CHARLIE
                  (whispering)
```
Right.  Exactly.  And  once  I  take  the  Lexus
back  it'll  start  being  like  it's  supposed
to  be.  Trust  me.
```

Like the scene between George and Doris, this scene too could be an unfunny argument. Arguments are not engaging and will not hold our attention unless the actors play games, register their wins and losses, and *enjoy* their wins.

Always keep in mind that when you play comedy you can go ridiculously far to get your own way. Look at Seinfeld episodes or the English sitcom, *Fawlty Towers*, or *The Office*. Notice how far the actors take their lines. The best actors physicalize their choices. They risk so much that their bodies unconsciously express their emotions. Take confrontations as far as you can. Play games if they are appropriate, and risk!

In this scene instead of Fighting to get your way about what to do, Fight to win the power in the marriage, so the argument becomes personal and has a history. This argument escalates to the point that Charlie tells Janet she is becoming hysterical. Each one tops the other. They have to come out on top. *Then* we have a riveting and hilarious scene.

                    CHARLIE
                   (to sky)
```
Help me.  This  is  a  perfect  time.  Right  now.
```

The more fervent you are, the funnier it will be. Differentiate each line from the last one. After the first two sentences, wait a Beat for God to answer your prayer. "Right now" should be tinged with impatience.

                    JANET
                  (whispers)
```
Charlie,  c'mere.
```

She says this urgently. Whispers can have drama and energy. Your stomach muscles should be tight because you are working so hard. She *orders* him over there.

                         CHARLIE
    What?

Remember, "What?" is never just a question. Here he says *Don't bother me!* with his "What?"

                         JANET
                       (whispers)
    SHSH! Look.

Janet tops him. Her SHSH says to Charlie, *I don't care what you were doing, be quiet and do what I say NOW.* It's a *loud* SHSH.

She stands looking around the bend in the road, pointing off —

JANET'S POV: A cabin about 100 yards off: parked between the porch and an old BMW is a BLACK LEXUS WITH A CRACKED REAR WINDOW.

Janet and Charlie take cover in the bushes.

                         CHARLIE
    Holy — !
                    (looks to sky)
    Thank you. See? Was that so hard?

TIP: *Whenever you ask a rhetorical question, wait for the answer with a small Beat before you continue talking. Never just ask a question. Never say "Huh?" or "What?" as though you have not heard. Give questions subtext and an action. Questions are often used to buy time.*

Charlie, after his Discovery that the Lexus is in front of them, is continuing his talk with God. Remember that Charlie was getting annoyed with God. After the first fervent "Thank you," he continues with that annoyance by asking God, "Was that so hard?" Take time to really commune with God.

                         JANET
                     (whispering)
    But no Emmett. And I don't see any
    motorcycle either. Let's go.

                         CHARLIE
                     (whispering)
    What about our Lexus?

Charlie does not just ask about the Lexus to remind Janet about it. He is chastising her for not remembering it. *You idiot* should be the subtext.

```
                    JANET
  We've got full coverage. They'll give us
  another one.
```

Janet tops him. Make sure this is not merely the exchange of information we talked about earlier. Each is calling the other one incompetent.

```
                   CHARLIE
  That's not the point.
```

When you're rehearsing a scene in which each partner is trying to obtain dominance over the other, include this exercise: Say "I win" after each line that you feel made a great point. Then don't forget the pleasure you take in winning. That exercise will be especially useful for this scene.

```
                    JANET
  Honey, we've got to find Emmett, remember?
  Remember Moose? Remember your knees? We're
  doing this for a reason, right, Charlie?
  Aren't we?
```

Janet calling him "Honey" should be through gritted teeth. Her reminding him of Moose, who is going to break Charlie's knees if he doesn't get the money, is not because Charlie has *forgotten*; it is because he's an idiot. Each "reminder" can come with a physical gesture such as a jab, and then Janet can top it by hitting him because he is so stupid. Each thought Janet has rises in importance above the last one. If the actress playing Janet does not go this far, then Charlie's reference to her getting hysterical will puzzle the audience.

```
                   CHARLIE
                 (whispering)
  Jan, you're getting hysterical. We catch
  Emmett faster and easier with the Lexus.
```

To some of us it might seem sensible to get help, especially as in the next line Janet refers to the nut case who has a gun and is willing to use it. Charlie should raise the stakes by having this Lexus be crazily important to him. Maybe it is the first luxury car he has ever had. Maybe he went to a huge amount of trouble to customize it. Make this car the most important thing in the world.

> JANET
> (whispering)
> Honey, this guy is nuts. He's got a loaded
> gun and he's willing to use it. Charlie,
> it's not supposed to be like this. I want
> a family. I want a home. I want my Mom to
> come visit us and the kids.

Janet becomes more hysterical as she realizes that Charlie might get them killed. Make sure her speech about the gun is not rushed. "He's got a loaded gun, *and* he's willing to *use* it." Separate the thoughts.

Suddenly and comically during the second part of the speech, Janet gives in to her fears about her future. She cries. She begs Charlie for comfort. When Janet breaks down, the scene changes. Her delivery is completely different. Take time between the two separate sections. The further she goes, begging Charlie for normalcy, the funnier the sudden change in attitude will be. Make the last word, *kids*, have an up-tilt.

> CHARLIE
> (whispering)
> Right. Exactly. And once I take the Lexus
> back it'll start being like it's supposed
> to be. Trust me.

Charlie's "Right" is happy. "Exactly" is even more excited. "Trust me" goes up in pitch so you don't end on a down note, which is fatal for this kind of comedy. Charlie has won, if only temporarily. We see his pleasure. But we also see the good part of their marriage and his tenderness.

Another comedic scene made funnier by risking and by choosing the best Fighting For is *The (Almost) Perfect Man* by screenwriter Bill Bigelow. Claire and her friend, Phillip (not a boyfriend), had foolishly walked into Central Park in New York at night. He had taken his gun, which he barely knew how to use. It went off, and when the police came they assumed that Claire had been attacked. Now Claire must protect the identity of her best friend, who ran away in a panic. She is at the police station being introduced to Annabel. It is important to know that Claire had described her ideal man to Phillip.

                    ANNABEL
      I'm a sketch artist.

                    CLAIRE
      A sketch artist?!

                    ANNABEL
      Your reaction's quite normal, Ma'am.
      You're probably worried that if you
      identify your assailant, the perpetrator
      of this heinous crime will enact some
      form of revenge. There's nothing to worry
      about. We'll protect you. A sketch doesn't
      take that long. We can do it in thirty to
      forty minutes tops.

                    CLAIRE
      But, but . . . but I can never remember a
      face. It's a real problem with me. I can
      meet someone one minute, then totally
      blank out the next.

                    ANNABEL
      It could prevent the next woman from
      being attacked.

                    CLAIRE
      I know, but I'm . . . I'm . . . I'm . . .
      You know it was dark. Very dark. Pitch
      black.

                    ANNABEL
      There's a full moon tonight.

                    CLAIRE
      Look. You have this all wrong.

                        ANNABEL
        It's okay, you just take your time. Let's
        start with this creep's hair. Was it
        curly or was it straight?

Claire blows off a breath. All she wants to do is get
out of there. She shoots them all a weak look, then —

                        CLAIRE
        Curly. Slightly receding.

Annabel hits some keys on the computer.

                        ANNABEL
        Like that?

                        CLAIRE
        Mm-hmm. That's close.

Annabel continues to work the computer, filling
in hair on an angular face. Claire stares at the
screen, her forehead creasing as she realizes she's
about to describe her old friend as the assailant.

                        CLAIRE
        Wait. No, no, no that's all wrong. I
        mean, his hair was . . .

There's a tiny beat as a tiny glint of intrigue
washes into Claire's eyes, then —

                        CLAIRE
        . . . long, dark, parted on the left side.

Annabel hits some keys.

                        ANNABEL
        More like that?

                        CLAIRE
        Yes, good. Really good. Only it hung over
        his eyebrow kind of cavalierly.

                        ANNABEL
        What about his jaw?

> CLAIRE
> Squared off. Like it was chiseled out of
> granite. Ice blue, piercing, slanted eyes . . .
> Sensuous mouth . . . Full nose . . .
> Mouth turned upward at the corners.

The face on the monitor fills in. Finally, at the
end of the MONTAGE —

> CLAIRE
> Oh, and he had a little scar under his
> right eye.

Annabel types into the keyboard.

> ANNABEL
> Like that?

> CLAIRE
> Perfect.

The first few lines are hard to make comedic or interesting. I gave this scene to two of my top professional students and yet when they started reading, I stopped them right away (or I would have fallen asleep). Look at Annabel's first line.

> ANNABEL
> I'm a sketch artist.

If she says it purely for information, it's dull. But if she says it gently yet cheerfully, with the Fighting For of soothing the obviously distraught and slightly nutty Claire, it has interesting subtext. It's funny if she sees Claire as someone who has to be treated like a mental patient.

> CLAIRE
> A sketch artist?!

This is a tricky line too. What Claire is really saying is, *Oh, no!!* She can make a Mistake here by almost screaming the line, or she can whisper it with equal horror. In any case she has to go far in order to justify Annabel's next line.

> ANNABEL
> Your reaction's quite normal, Ma'am.

But Claire's reaction is *not* normal, so Annabel should take a moment to register that and to think up a soothing falsehood before she says the line. Then Annabel (Ahhhh!) makes a Discovery about why Claire is so freaked out. Take a moment to make that Discovery.

> ANNABEL (CONT)
> You're probably worried that if you
> identify your assailant, the perpetrator
> of this heinous crime will enact some
> form of revenge. There's nothing to worry
> about. We'll protect you. A sketch doesn't
> take that long. We can do it in thirty to
> forty minutes tops.

When Annabel's line about protecting Claire doesn't convince her, Annabel comes up with the line about it not taking too long. Of course you won't run all those lines together, but will make them specific.

> CLAIRE
> But, but . . . but I can never remember a
> face. It's a real problem with me. I can
> meet someone one minute, then totally
> blank out the next.

The harder Claire works to get out of her predicament, the harder we'll laugh. Each "but" must have a real thought after it, a big struggle to think of an excuse. Take your time and work! Finally Claire is happy to have thought of a terrific excuse. You might even physicalize seeing the face of someone and then that face being wiped out. Go far. Risk! This is a comedy.

> ANNABEL
> It could prevent the next woman from
> being attacked.

> CLAIRE
> I know, but I'm . . . I'm . . . I'm . . .
> You know it was dark. Very dark. Pitch
> black.

After each "I'm . . ." we should see Claire's entire body involved and working hard as she tries to come up with excuses. Then she thinks of the best excuse yet. Hooray! She's happy to have thought of it, and that should show. It was not only dark; top it with "*very* dark" and then top that with "pitch black." Each image should be different and rise in importance over the other line.

> ANNABEL
> There's a full moon tonight.

Annabel should take a fraction of a second to figure out how to politely but flatly contradict Claire, as if there is an "uh" before the line. Annabel can talk slowly, as if to an idiot, and even ridiculously point to the window or the ceiling to show that full moon.

> CLAIRE
> Look. You have this all wrong.

Claire has blown it with the too-dark-to-see excuse, so she thinks she'd better confess. She takes on a whole new attitude. (She "starts the scene over.") Annabel interrupts her and then Claire becomes caught up in creating images on the monitor.

> ANNABEL
> It's okay, you just
> take your time. Let's
> start with this creep's
> hair. Was it curly or
> was it straight?

TIP: *Whenever it is appropriate, abruptly take an entirely new tone. We do it in life. We see that a negotiation is not going well so we say, "Okay, okay, let's begin again," or, "Okay, that approach is not working; let's try this one." This tactic grabs the attention of your partner and the audience. I call it* **starting the scene over.** *Look for places in your scene where you can start over.*

Annabel should illustrate for Claire the image of curly and straight hair by making little curls with her hands, perhaps. Remember that Annabel thinks she needs to give slow and careful explanations to Claire. (Also remember a point made earlier: don't create fake images for the audience; create images for your partner to help him/her see what you are talking about. We do it in real life all the time.)

When Annabel creates the face on the computer Claire should get caught up in seeing Phillip emerge.

> CLAIRE
> Mm-hmm. That's close.

She should almost be saying, *Wow!* as she is fascinated by the process and gets carried away by it. Suddenly she is brought back to reality as she realizes she is implicating her friend.

> CLAIRE
> Wait. No, no, no that's all wrong. I
> mean, his hair was . . .

A good director could get a laugh with a close-up of Annabel looking oddly at Claire. "Huh?" her expression would be saying.

There's a tiny beat as a tiny glint of intrigue washes into Claire's eyes, then —

Claire begins describing her ideal man. The one she described earlier to her friend. The comedy comes now from Claire falling in love with the image she is creating. Each image makes her fall harder.

> CLAIRE
> Ice blue, piercing, slanted eyes . . .
> Sensuous mouth . . . Full nose . . .
> Mouth turned upward at the corners.

The face on the monitor fills in. Finally, at the end of the MONTAGE —

Claire is in love with the image. Now, she adds just the right touch—

> CLAIRE
> Oh, and he had a little scar under his
> right eye.

Annabel types into the keyboard.

> ANNABEL
> Like that?

> CLAIRE
> Perfect.

Before the last line Claire should take a long moment. She says "per-fect" as a woman transformed by love. (She is so in love that she swipes a copy of the sketch.)

Summary

To be funny you have to have comedic timing and a comedic atti-tude. You have to dare to risk and you have to take the situation you are in very, very seriously. In broad comedies you must generate enough excitement to create a fast pace and an up-tilt at the ends of most sentences. You have to get huge pleasure out of topping and scoring points. You have to be amused by your partner and learn game-playing. Some lucky actors have a natural ability for comedy, but for most it is a learned skill that takes years to master.

8   **Script Analysis**

How to Get the Most out of Every Script

In the following section I analyze scenes from film and theater. Read the scene first and make your own choices. After you break down the scene, read my analysis to see if you could have gone further.

Look for ways to make your performance rise above the obvious. Look for a strong Fighting For, Beats, humor, a delight in your wins, topping, a strong need to be in the scene, a fascination with your partner, high stakes, and a complex subtext under the lines. Strong, exciting, and specific choices make your work fascinating.

This beautifully written scene from the screenplay *The Hours*, adapted by David Hare, takes place between Richard, who is dying of AIDS, and Clarissa, who has taken care of him obsessively for years, neglecting her own family and her lover, Sally, in the process. In the past Clarissa and Richard were lovers.

                        RICHARD
I think I'm only staying alive to
satisfy you.

                    CLARISSA
So? Well? That's what we do. That's what
people do. They stay alive for each other.
The doctors told you, you don't need to
die. The doctors told you that. You can
live like this for years.

                    RICHARD
Well, exactly.

                    CLARISSA
I don't accept this. I don't accept what
you're saying.

                    RICHARD
Oh what? And it's you to decide is it?

                    CLARISSA
No.

                    RICHARD
How long have you been doing this?

                    CLARISSA
Doing what?

                    RICHARD
How many years, coming to this apartment?
What about your own life? What about
Sally? Just wait till I die. Then you'll
have to think of yourself.

Clarissa doesn't answer. Richard smiles, sure of
his point.

                    RICHARD
How are you going to like that?

Clarissa lets go of his hand, disturbed. RICHARD
just looks at her. CLARISSA gets up and stands a
moment, shaken. Then speaks quietly.

                    CLARISSA
Richard, it would be great if you did come.
If you felt well enough to come. Just to

```
        let you know: I'm making the crab thing.
        Not that I imagine it makes any difference.

                        RICHARD
        Of course it makes a difference. I love
        the crab thing.

CLARISSA is about to leave but RICHARD calls across
to her.

                        RICHARD
        Clarissa?

                        CLARISSA
        Yes?

RICHARD raises his head slightly for her to kiss
him. Clarissa puts her lips next to his with great
tenderness, not to hurt him. Then she squeezes
his shoulder.

                        CLARISSA
        I'll come back at three-thirty to help
        you get dressed.

                        RICHARD
        Wonderful.

CLARISA goes out.

                        RICHARD
        Wonderful.
```

Read this scene several times to figure out what each person is Fighting For. One of my students originally thought Richard was Fighting to die.

Another thought Clarissa was Fighting to keep him alive because she can't stand the thought of life without him. Also, she doesn't have to examine her life if she is busy taking care of Richard's.

Clarissa's Fighting For was fine. It is strong and the stakes are high, especially if you choose that she is terrified of life without Richard and feels she will collapse without his support.

But if Richard is only Fighting to die, then Clarissa is not important enough in the scene. Remember, your Fighting For must be *about the other person in the scene* or you will look self-centered.

Remember also that you must use your own intelligence in every scene. What you know, your character knows. Richard knows very well what an unhealthy importance he has in Clarissa's life. In the past he may even have exploited it. Now he wants to die, yet he loves Clarissa. He knows what his death will do to her.

A better Fighting For is for him to help Clarissa accept his death. This way we will see Richard's love and compassion, his tact and his gratitude. Instead of a selfish man who only thinks about his desire to die, we will see a sensitive and compassionate man wanting to help someone he loves accept his death.

> RICHARD
> I think I'm only staying alive to
> satisfy you.

This line should create a Beat as Clarissa receives the hurtful words. Richard knows he is broaching a sensitive and hurtful topic. He is gentle and loving as he tries to do it in the best way for Clarissa. After the Beat Clarissa overcomes her shock and tries to talk him out of his "mood" (as she sees it).

> CLARISSA
> So? Well? That's what we do. That's what
> people do. They stay alive for each other.
> The doctors told you, you don't need to
> die. The doctors told you that. You can
> live like this for years.

Clarissa is panicked by Richard's talking about dying. She doesn't want to open that can of worms. Notice how she repeats herself. Notice how desperate she sounds and how high the stakes are for her.

> RICHARD
> Well, exactly.

Here Richard can use gentle humor to make her see that living "like this" is not a good choice for him. Separate the *well* from the *exactly* to make the point stronger.

> CLARISSA
> I don't accept this. I don't accept what you're saying.

Clarissa's panic goes up a notch. She has to be even stronger to make Richard be quiet, or to blot out what he is saying by the force of her will. Don't make the two sentences sound alike.

> RICHARD
> Oh what? And it's you to decide is it?

Richard makes a Mistake here. He loses his temper briefly. Clarissa should take her time to answer. (Beat) She understands he means he is the only one who can decide about his death. This is a difficult admission for Clarissa as it makes her feel helpless.

> CLARISSA
> No.

Richard calms down immediately. He feels sorry for Clarissa, who is upset at the thought of losing him and feeling helpless to do anything about it.

> RICHARD
> How long have you been doing this?

Richard is nudging her to acceptance again. He can be gentle and sweet and use a little humor.

> CLARISSA
> Doing what?

Don't fall in to the trap of thinking Clarissa hasn't heard him or doesn't know what he means. Clarissa is a brilliant woman and she knows exactly what he means. Her question is only asked to put off answering him.

(Remember that when your line is a question like Clarissa's, or "What?" or "Huh?" never think the character has not heard or has not understood. Questions are usually asked to buy time. There is always subtext in questions.)

                    RICHARD
    How many years, coming to this apartment?
    What about your own life? What about
    Sally? Just wait till I die. Then you'll
    have to think of yourself.

Clarissa doesn't answer. She is terrified and doesn't want to answer these questions. They touch on her romantic feelings about Richard and her neurotic dependency on him.

                    RICHARD
    How are you going to like that?

Clarissa lets go of his hand, disturbed. RICHARD
just looks at her. CLARISSA gets up and stands a
moment, shaken. Then speaks quietly.

The blocking shown here is from the movie. What Richard is saying is so difficult for Clarissa to face that she literally can't sit still. She is on the verge of tears. She gets up. She may find some chore to do to calm herself. (Remember that your use of props reflects your emotions.) Then she firmly changes the subject. When Richard asks, "How are you going to like that?" he should not be nasty or sarcastic. He is asking with interest. He is nudging her toward facing facts. Clarissa doesn't answer Richard's question. She can't—yet. So she changes the subject.

                    CLARISSA
    Richard, it would be great if you did come.
    If you felt well enough to come. Just to
    let you know: I'm making the crab thing.
    Not that I imagine it makes any difference.

Clarissa can laugh at herself for thinking the "crab thing" would make a difference. But Richard knows she has had enough. He's content he at least raised the subject and got her thinking about his death. For now he will just comfort her and show appreciation for all she does for him.

                    RICHARD
    Of course it makes a difference. I love
    the crab thing.

CLARISSA is about to leave but RICHARD calls across
to her.

> RICHARD
>
> Clarissa?

Richard wants to see her leave happily. He doesn't want to worry
about her after she leaves. So he calls her over to give her a kiss.

> CLARISSA
>
> Yes?

RICHARD raises his head slightly for her to kiss
him. Clarissa puts her lips next to his with great
tenderness, not to hurt him. Then she squeezes
his shoulder.

Clarissa hopes the whole subject is behind them. She hopes he will
never bring it up again. She acts now as if nothing is wrong. She is
cheerful and brisk and efficient. If this is your only scene as Clarissa for
an audition, the auditors will be impressed to see so many sides of you.

> CLARISSA
>
> I'll come back at three-thirty to help
> you get dressed.

> RICHARD
>
> Wonderful.

"Wonderful" is Richard's gift to Clarissa. It should be said whole-
heartedly, with no sarcasm, to make her happy.

CLARISA goes out.

> RICHARD
>
> Wonderful.

The final "Wonderful" is in complete contrast to the first. Don't let
yourself be *just* sarcastic or nasty. This "Wonderful" should show how
alone Richard feels, and how trapped by his responsibility for Clarissa.
We should sense his vulnerability, pain, and fear.

The Subject Was Roses

The following scene from *The Subject Was Roses*, by Frank D. Gilroy, is one of my favorites because although the husband and wife both want to save their marriage, their Fighting Fors are at cross-purposes. Nettie and John argue all the time. They are miserable. Their son, just home from war, has sent flowers to his mother, telling her they were from the father. This simple act has the power to change the parents' relationship—if they let it.

As you read the scene, figure out what each actor is fighting for. Nettie and John fight hard for their wants and they each have specific terms they demand. What are they? What is the obstacle each role faces? Make a choice before you read the analysis.

NETTIE: Home two days and both nights to bed like that.

JOHN: He's entitled. You should hear some of the things he's been through. They overran one of those concentration camps —

NETTIE: I don't want to hear about it now.

JOHN: You're right. It's no way to end a happy evening.

NETTIE: I think we have some aspirin in the kitchen.

She moves into the kitchen. He follows; watches her take a bottle of aspirin from counter drawer.

JOHN: You didn't say anything before about a headache.

NETTIE: I don't have a headache.

JOHN: Then what —

NETTIE: I read that if you put an aspirin in cut flowers they keep longer.

She drops an aspirin in the vase; regards the roses.

NETTIE: I wonder what made you get them?

JOHN: I don't know.

NETTIE: There must have been some reason.

Nettie smells them.

JOHN: I just thought it would be nice to do.
NETTIE: It was.

(They regard each other a moment.)

JOHN: I like your dress.
NETTIE: You've seen it before.
JOHN: It looks different . . . Everything about you looks different.
NETTIE: (Turns to him) What mass are you going to?
JOHN: Ten o'clock.
NETTIE: I better set the alarm.
JOHN: Nettie? I had a good time tonight.
NETTIE: So did I.

Nettie enters the living room and places the roses on coffee table; arranges them.

JOHN: Did you really? Or were you putting it on for his sake?
NETTIE: I really did.
JOHN: So did I.

Nettie crosses to chair and picks up Timmy's jacket.

NETTIE: I'll set the alarm for nine-fifteen.
JOHN: Now that he's back we'll have lots of good times.
NETTIE: What's wrong between you and I has nothing to do with him.
JOHN: I didn't say it did.
NETTIE: We have to solve our own problems.
JOHN: Of course.
NETTIE: They can't be solved in one night.
JOHN: I know.
NETTIE: One nice evening doesn't make everything different.

John puts his arm around her waist.

JOHN: Did I say it did?

His lips brush the nape of her neck.

NETTIE: I guess you don't understand.

John kisses her neck.

NETTIE: You'll spoil everything.

John squeezes her waist.

   JOHN: I want things right between us.
NETTIE: You think this is going to make them right?

John's hands move to her breasts.

   JOHN: We have to start someplace.

Nettie breaks away.

NETTIE: Start?
   JOHN: Bless us and save us.
NETTIE: That's not my idea of a start.
   JOHN: Nettie, I want you . . . I want you like I
        never wanted anything in my life.
NETTIE: Stop.
   JOHN: Please?
NETTIE: You're drunk.
   JOHN: *Do you think I could ask again if I wasn't?*
NETTIE: I'm not one of your hotel-lobby whores.
   JOHN: If you were I wouldn't have to ask.
NETTIE: A couple of drinks, a couple of jokes, and
        let's jump in bed.
   JOHN: Maybe that's my mistake.
NETTIE: How do you suppose Ruskin managed without
        you today?
   JOHN: Maybe you don't want to be asked. (he
        seizes her)
NETTIE: Let me alone.
   JOHN: (as they struggle at couch) *You've had the*
        drinks. You've had the jokes.
NETTIE: Stop!

She breaks free of him, regards him for a moment,
then picks up the vase of roses and hurls them
against the floor.

(Remember to read the scene again and decide on what each character is Fighting For before reading the analysis that follows).

They are both Fighting to get the love back between them. But they have different terms. I love the almost mathematical equation:

JOHN: Wants Nettie to prove her love. TERMS: By having sex now.

NETTIE: Wants John to prove his love. TERMS: By waiting to have sex.

Read the scene again and see how John and Nettie maneuver to get what they want. They are each hurt and furious when their wants are not understood.

Nettie wants to be wooed. She'll give him sex, but not so fast. Not until they talk and get some things straight and until she feels good about the relationship. This process might take days or weeks. Nettie thinks John should *prove he cares by being willing to wait for sex until she is ready.*

John thinks Nettie should *prove her love by having sex tonight* now that the atmosphere is different between them. After all, she thinks he sent her flowers and he didn't tell her differently. There is something new in the atmosphere. If Nettie loves him she should prove it by giving him the gift of sex.

The scene begins with them fighting about their son, Timmy, going to bed drunk for the second time in two nights. Then Nettie says something important.

NETTIE: I don't want to hear about it now.

John picks up on the *now.* John sees the possibility for a positive change and romance hanging in the air. He's excited.

    JOHN: You're right. It's no way to end a happy
           evening.

"You're right" is a big Discovery. John thinks the relationship could be turned around tonight. They could have sex. He's excited.

John's hopes are dashed when Nettie asks for an aspirin. The actress playing Nettie must use her intelligence and *know* what John is talking about when he is anxious about the aspirin: *Not tonight, dear, I have a headache.*

NETTIE: I wonder what made you get them.

Here Nettie becomes vulnerable. As the actress, you should know specifically what words she wants to hear from John. "Because I love you," perhaps?

There is a BEAT while John thinks of what to say.

JOHN: I don't know.

Nettie registers her disappointment with a Beat. She could leave it here and go to bed but she doesn't. She gives John another opening by asking again why he gave her the flowers.

NETTIE: There must have been some reason.

Beat.

For a second, John can't think of the right thing to say. He even has the option of coming clean and telling her Timmy bought them.

JOHN: I just thought it would be nice to do.
NETTIE: It was.

HUGE BEAT. Things are different now. They have laid their cards out on the table. They look at each other and see possibilities. They both want the love back between them.

JOHN: I like your dress.

Nettie is wary of the compliment. She spends the next lines walking away from John, avoiding his touch, because she knows he'll want to make love and, as she says, it will "spoil everything." Note how she bustles around getting things ready for the next day. Her words are appreciative, but all her blocking and her handling of the props say *Don't touch me*. The tragedy is that John doesn't get the message.

John follows Nettie all over the room trying to get close to her. He thinks if only he makes love to her, their relationship will get back on track.

NETTIE: One nice evening doesn't make everything
          different.
JOHN: Did I say it did?

They sound as if they are communicating, but Nettie's warning messages are not getting across. Nettie says their problems "can't be solved in one night," and "One nice evening doesn't make everything different."

John doesn't understand that she is warning him to wait to ask for sex, and he tries to seduce her to show his love. Nettie gets more and more agitated as she keeps giving John messages he doesn't get: telling him, shrugging him off, and walking away from him. John works hard to seduce her by giving her compliments, begging her, and touching her.

```
NETTIE:  That's not my idea of a start.
  JOHN:  Nettie, I want you . . . I want you like I
         never wanted anything in my life.
NETTIE:  Stop!
```

Nettie can't make herself any clearer. She has told him what she wants (she thinks), and he doesn't care (she thinks), so for her the experiment is over.

```
NETTIE:  You're drunk.
```

She insults him. She punishes him. And John comes right back with his next line.

```
  JOHN:  Do you think I could ask again if I wasn't?
```

The italics are the playwright's; they are used to show how high the stakes are. The line shows how hard it was for John to try again after so many rejections. The actor should realize how high the hurdle was John had to jump. The actor has to work hard.

```
NETTIE:  I'm not one of your hotel-lobby whores.
```

Nettie is again telling him she needs to be treated differently. She needs to be wooed. She wants John to see her as special, not just as a sex object. Also maybe she knows or suspects John used "whores." How galling that must be for Nettie.

```
  JOHN:  If you were I wouldn't have to ask.
```

John is confirming (whether it is true or not) that he uses whores. He says it to punish Nettie.

JOHN: Maybe you don't want to be asked.

The subtext is *Maybe you want to be forced.* John grabs Nettie to force her.

JOHN: *You've had the drinks. You've had the jokes.*

(The playwright again uses italics to show importance, so *risk* getting really angry.) To hurt her, John puts Nettie at the level of the whores she accused him of using.

John is at his wit's end. He insults her the way she insulted him. They punish each other for not understanding each other's Fighting Fors. He implies she is not worth more than a few drinks and a few jokes. She hurls the vase of flowers she thinks he gave her.

Beat.

The roses symbolized their last chance to save their marriage. Now they look at each other knowing their marriage is beyond hope. The moment is huge for both

> **TIP:** *Each time your Fighting For is thwarted, the stakes are raised.*

of them. They each had a different agenda with the same end (love) but different terms (sex/no sex), and neither understood the other.

What to Do with a Scene that Seems Corny

We are corny in life. Some of the things you've said would make you blush if they weren't completely sincere. If you say something you know is corny, you laugh at yourself or apologize for the way you expressed it and add, "but I really mean it anyway."

Often plays or screenplays written in the 1930s or 40s have dialogue that sounds *really* corny at first glance, but when it is done correctly you see that it has power.

One of my favorite scenes is *Still Life* by Noel Coward, a famous play from the 1930s, which was turned into an even more famous film called *Brief Encounter* with Trevor Howard and Celia Johnson. I had my class work on the famous scene in a railway station in which the characters, married to others in the days when divorce was rare, are never going to see each other again. Alec is going to Africa with his wife.

                         ALEC
Are you all right, darling?

                         LAURA
Yes, I'm all right.

                         ALEC
I wish I could think of something to say.

                         LAURA
It doesn't matter — not saying anything
I mean.

                         ALEC
I'll miss my train and wait to see you
into yours.

                         LAURA
No — no — please don't. I'll come over
to your platform with you — I'd rather.

                         ALEC
Very well.

                         LAURA
Do you think we shall ever see each
other again?

                         ALEC
I don't know.
               (his voice breaks)
Not for years anyway.

                         LAURA
The children will all be grown up — I
wonder if they'll ever meet and know
each other.

                         ALEC
Couldn't I write to you — just once in
a while?

                         LAURA
No — please not — we promised we wouldn't.

ALEC

Please know this — please know that you'll
be with me for ages and ages yet — far
away into the future. Time will wear
down the agony of not seeing you, bit by
bit the pain will go — but the loving you
and the memory of you won't ever go —
please know that.

LAURA

I know it.

ALEC

It's easier for me than for you. I do
realize that, really I do. I at least
will have different shapes to look at,
and new work to do — you have to go on
among familiar things — my heart aches
for you.

LAURA

I'll be all right.

ALEC

I love you with all my heart and soul.

LAURA
(quietly)
I want to die — if only I could die.

ALEC

If you died you'd forget me — I want to
be remembered.

LAURA

Yes, I know — I do too.

ALEC

Good-bye, my dearest love.

LAURA

Good-bye, my dearest love.

```
                    ALEC
     We've still got a few minutes.


                    LAURA
     Thank God.

(Dolly Messiter bustles into the refreshment room.
She sees Laura)

                    DOLLY
     Laura! What a lovely surprise.
```

I had pairs of students read this scene, and the whole class was soon laughing (including me, the teacher, I must admit) at the students' desperate attempts to say the lines without cracking up.

Alec's speech was especially difficult: "Please know this — please know that you'll be with me for ages and ages yet — far away into the future. Time will wear down the agony of not seeing you, bit by bit the pain will go — but the loving you and the memory of you will never go — please know that."

To present-day students this speech sounded hilarious. What was the solution? One tremendous help was the addition of humor. Not "hah hah" humor, but the gentle humor of someone who knows he's being corny, but means what he says.

It was necessary for the actors to be aware of the importance of the scene. Realizing it was the last time Alec and Laura would see each other made the words come out slowly and painfully, and they became real.

Every line must be specific. For example, "The loving you" and "the memory of you" must not sound the same. The loving and the memory must be thought up individually. The word *agony*, in "Time will wear down the agony of not seeing you," can sound excruciatingly corny unless Alec searches for the word. He doesn't know how to put it. He pauses a split second to think of a perfect word. Now "agony" doesn't sound corny, because it is exactly what he means.

This speech is his final gift to her. Each word is carefully thought out. He wants it to be perfect for her to make her remember him. He takes time. The speech is broken up. He pauses for just the perfect way to put things. The stakes are enormous.

When Laura falls apart, she makes one of the Mistakes I have discussed, and for a second she loses control. "I want to die — if only I could die," she says. Look at Alec's reply: "If you died you'd forget me — I want to be remembered." Can't you see Alec saying it with a gentle laugh and Laura sucking up her Mistake and giving him a rueful smile?

Laura's lines were difficult to make real until we added that she is barely holding herself together from collapsing into tears. In England in those days people did *not* indulge in emotion in train stations. Laura is working hard to stay in control.

Alec offers to miss his train and see Laura to hers. Laura answers, "No — no — please don't. I'll come over to your platform with you — I'd rather." Most of the students made her sound like a dying duck, or whiny and exhausted. But when we added the fact that she was trying to control her tears, which were threatening to spill out, it became obvious that Alec's suggestion that he change the plans and see her to her train threatened that control and made her panic. She had to work hard to make him realize she couldn't stand a change of plan. That seeing him for much longer would be unbearable and threaten her control. Saying, "No — no — please don't" with urgency and high stakes added reality and poignancy.

Alec says toward the end of the scene, "I love you with all my heart and soul." Dialogue about souls these days, especially loving someone with your soul, can be hard to say. What to do? Alec must say the line "I love you with all my heart" and then pause. It doesn't seem enough to express all his emotions, and so after an infinitesimal pause he adds the words *and soul*. The high stakes and the need to give her the gift of his words make the lines believable.

After we worked on this scene by raising the stakes and making each word specific, the scene changed dramatically. Before the changes the class was laughing hysterically; after the changes everyone wiped away tears (including the teacher).

How to Add Colors to a Scene

Shadowlands, by William Nicholson, is a prizewinning play and screenplay. The film starred Anthony Hopkins and Debra Winger. This moving true story is about the writer C. S. Lewis, a painfully shy and emotionally stunted Englishman who falls in love with an American divorced woman. He had married her in name only, ostensibly to allow her to stay in the country, but he falls in love with her. Before he can reveal his love, she is diagnosed with terminal bone cancer. This scene takes place in the hospital just after a doctor told Lewis (whose nickname was Jack) the grim prognosis. Joy suspects how serious her illness is.

LEWIS: They're going to operate on the broken hip tomorrow.

JOY: I'm sorry, Jack. I didn't mean you to have all this bother.

LEWIS: Tush, woman. You're the one who's having the bother.

JOY: What I mean is, I don't expect you to worry about me.

LEWIS: Oh? And who do you expect to worry about you?

JOY: You know what I am trying to say.

LEWIS: Who else should be worrying about you but me? You are my wife.

JOY: Technically.

LEWIS: Then I shall worry about you technically.

JOY: Just how much do I have to worry about, Jack? They won't tell me.

LEWIS: That's because they aren't sure themselves.

JOY: Tell me, Jack.

LEWIS: I don't know any more than they do, Joy.

JOY: Please.

(pause)

LEWIS: They expect you to die.

JOY: Thank you.

(Having got what she wanted, she pauses to regain strength. Then:)

JOY: What do you say, Jack? I'm a Jew. Divorced. Broke. And I'm dying of cancer. Do I get a discount?

LEWIS: I don't want to lose you, Joy.

JOY: I don't want to be lost . . . You know something? You seem different. You look at me properly now.

```
LEWIS:  Didn't I before?
  JOY:  Not properly.
LEWIS:  Would you give me your hand?
```

(She gives him her hand. He holds it and strokes it.)

```
  JOY:  Can I say anything I want, Jack?
LEWIS:  Yes.
  JOY:  Anything?
LEWIS:  Yes.
  JOY:  You know it anyway.
LEWIS:  Yes.
  JOY:  I'm still going to say it.
LEWIS:  You say it.
  JOY:  I love you, Jack.
```

(He seems about to respond with a declaration of his own, but it does not quite come out)

```
LEWIS:  Better now?
  JOY:  Better. Do you mind?
LEWIS:  No.
```

(A spasm of pain passes through her.)

(Lewis watches Joy in pain. He can't bear it. He goes looking for the Nurse)

```
LEWIS:  Nurse! Nurse!
```

At first reading you might not expect to find humor and jokes and secret messages, but they're all there to add poignancy and depth. Read it again. Look for the places that could have different colors, and only then read the analysis that follows.

```
LEWIS:  They're going to operate on the broken hip
        tomorrow.
```

If you say this first line with the intention of *just* giving information, you have missed an opportunity. Don't forget that your first line has to have an action. In this case the action could be to divert Joy from thinking about the cancer by making her think only about the broken hip. (Maybe Jack needs the diversion more than Joy.) So Jack's line could be said with optimism and cheer, as if once the broken hip is fixed then all else will be well.

>   JOY: I'm sorry, Jack. I didn't mean you to have
>   all this bother.

Joy is intelligent and she knows her sickness might force Jack to invest more in the relationship than he is ready for. She wanted to take it slower. Her cancer has pushed them into a new intimacy. The word *bother* is important because it has to substitute for all this knowledge.

>   LEWIS: Tush, woman. You're the one who's having
>   the bother.

Lewis is uncomfortable talking about it, so he pushes it aside with a mild joke. He must smile at his own joke. She can smile too before she attempts to give the message again by slightly rephrasing it.

>   JOY: What I mean is, I don't expect you to worry
>   about me.
>   LEWIS: Oh? And who do you expect to worry about you?

Again Lewis pushes away what Joy is saying with a joke. So she tells him she knows that he knows with the next line.

>   JOY: You know what I am trying to say.

Lewis can no longer pretend not to understand. This is a big moment for him and he now reveals his love to Joy *for the first time*. He takes a moment before he says it to give her the message that he is saying something momentous.

>   LEWIS: Who else should be worrying about you but
>   me? You are my wife.

The first line is acknowledging how important their relationship is. The next line is even more important. Again Lewis should pause before he says it. They are married in name only, but with this line he tells her he loves her—that he accepts her as his true wife. This sentence "You are my wife" is romantic and should be said as a declaration of love and commitment.

Joy receives this declaration with understanding. She knows its importance. To lighten the moment, and perhaps as a gift to Jack, who is uncomfortable with emotions, she makes a small joke of her own.

```
  JOY:    Technically.
LEWIS:    Then I shall worry about you technically.
```

Jack acknowledges the joke and makes one of his own, but the sub-text must be that he confirms his intention of accepting her as a true wife. They share a moment of love and intimacy and knowledge about how far their relationship has come. This gives Joy the courage to ask Jack the truth about her health.

```
  JOY:    Just how much do I have to worry about,
          Jack? They won't tell me.
LEWIS:    That's because they aren't sure themselves.
```

Jack is not telling her what he knows, because he can't bear to. Remember that actors must lie well. Joy sees though the lie, however.

```
  JOY:    Tell me, Jack.
```

It takes courage for Joy not to accept the lie. We should admire her strength. She should say the line with no sentimentality.

```
LEWIS:    I don't know any more than they do, Joy.
```

Again Lewis can't bear to tell her. Again he tries hard but fails to convince her. Maybe Joy has heard something from the nurses or doctors. She *knows* but she wants to have it confirmed.

```
  JOY:    Please.
```

(pause)

The pause, written by the playwright, is for Jack to gather up his courage and to realize she won't be content with anything less than the truth. After her line Joy keeps giving strong silent messages encouraging him to tell her.

```
LEWIS:    They expect you to die.
```

After this terrible message Lewis should send a silent, more hopeful, message about how he will be there for her.

```
  JOY:    Thank you.
```

Joy has to take a moment to absorb this terrible blow, but then Joy's gratitude is strong because she knows how much it cost Lewis to tell her. Her gift to him is to make another joke to lighten the atmosphere.

(Having got what she wanted, she pauses to regain strength. Then:)

> JOY: What do you say, Jack? I'm a Jew. Divorced.
>   Broke. And I'm dying of cancer. Do I get
>   a discount?

The joke doesn't work on Lewis. He is too overcome with emotion. He can barely keep it together.

> LEWIS: I don't want to lose you, Joy.

This is Jack's first overt declaration of how much Joy means to him. He must be pushing back tears. Joy understands and she tells him she too feels as terrible as he does. She replies, "I don't want to be lost," which has a double meaning—she doesn't want to die, and she doesn't want to lose their love. It is her return declaration of love, a safer one than using the word *love*. After that line she takes a Beat, and then she makes a wonderful Discovery.

> JOY: I don't want to be lost . . . You know
>   something? You seem different. You look at
>   me properly now.

Make sure, if you are playing Joy, you make the Discovery *this very moment*—the Discovery that Lewis is looking at her as a lover instead of a (scared) friend.

> LEWIS: Didn't I before?
>   JOY: Not properly.

Joy means he had never before looked at her with romantic love. This is a further acknowledgement of how things have changed between them.

> LEWIS: Would you give me your hand?

Lewis asks for the first time to touch her as a lover would. This is understood by them both. The touch is significant to them both.

(She gives him her hand. He holds it and strokes it.) Silent and important messages are exchanged before she decides to take things one step further.

    JOY: Can I say anything I want, Jack?

She and Jack know she wants to tell him she loves him. (Remember that actors should not play dumb. They should get things as fast as or faster than the audience.)

LEWIS: Yes.

This "Yes" is brave and difficult for the emotionally terrified Lewis.

    JOY: Anything?
LEWIS: Yes.
    JOY: You know it anyway.
LEWIS: Yes.
    JOY: I'm still going to say it.

The line of Lewis' that follows is not just giving her permission to say the scary words. It should also be cheerleading for her to say it. It should be as if he is saying, "You go for it, girl." He says it with emphasis.

LEWIS: You say it.

Joy takes a Beat before she says the next line.

    JOY: I love you, Jack.

(He seems about to respond with a declaration of his own, but it does not quite come out)

We should see Lewis struggle to say "I love you" in return. Again Joy can send him a silent message of encouragement. He takes time to try forcing the words out, but he is too afraid. Instead he says something relatively meaningless.

LEWIS: Better now?

Joy is happy she told him and she understands he tried. She feels loving and not hurt, but still she needs reassurance she didn't go too far.

    JOY: Better. Do you mind?

Don't run these sentences together. First, Joy answers the meaningless phrase, "Better now?" She could smile at him with understanding of the silly words. Then she has a moment of anxiety. Maybe he didn't like it that she told him she loved him. She needs reassurance so she asks, "Do you mind?"

LEWIS: No.

He doesn't mind that she told him. The subtext of this is he is happy that she had the courage. He says it with strength, and she can see his love.

(A spasm of pain passes through her.)

(Lewis watches Joy in pain. He can't bear it. He goes looking for the Nurse)

LEWIS: Nurse! Nurse!

Perhaps Lewis registers relief that he doesn't have to deal with what feels to him like emotional minefields. Now he can take action and escape by summoning the nurse. Doing something concrete to help Joy is much easier for him than talking to her about his feelings.

The Trap of Anger

The following partial scene is from the play *Jesus Hopped the A Train* by Stephen Adly Guirgis. Actors who fall into the trap of anger will appear to be doing nothing more than shouting. They won't reveal other dimensions. The scene could become so one-note that the audience will tune out. Anger is the easiest emotion for actors to play, but unless they add vulnerability and communication, they are not appealing to their partners, the audience, or the casting directors. Read the following scene between Angel, an incarcerated criminal, and his lawyer, Mary Jane. As you read it, look for the growing relationship between them and look for areas of vulnerability and pain.

Manhattan Correctional Center, legal consultations room. Mary Jane and Angel (beaten up) midstream:

ANGEL: — What I want is a fuckin' lawyer!! Is
         it possible, in this nightmare — I mean,
         what the fuck is this?! Even on TV they
         get a lawyer —

MARY JANE:	I am a lawyer. I am your lawyer —
ANGEL:	I wanna real lawyer.
MARY JANE:	I am a real lawyer and you are my real client. —
ANGEL:	Fuck that!
MARY JANE:	You wanna see the paperwork?
ANGEL:	Fuck the paperwork! Why didn't you check the paperwork before you come in here talking all kinda shit when you didn't even know who you was speakin' to?
MARY JANE:	Look I am sorry for the mix-up, I —
ANGEL:	The "mix-up"? Is that what happened before? Or do you just never know who anybody is?
MARY JANE:	I'm sorry.
ANGEL:	I ain't Hector Villanueva!!
MARY JANE:	I know that —
ANGEL:	Hector Villanueva, NO Aqui!!
MARY JANE:	OK, what I need from you —
ANGEL:	Need?! You gonna sit and talk to me about what you need? I'm incarcerated, lady! Why can't we talk about what I fuckin' need?!
MARY JANE:	What do you need?
ANGEL:	I need a damn lawyer!
MARY JANE:	Which is why I'm here —
ANGEL:	This is bullshit! This is racism is what it is, racism!! If I was white, I'd have a motherfuckin' Perry Mason sittin' here wit' the little glasses and the beard talking fuckin' strategy. Instead they give me some bumbling'-ass Wilma Flintstone don't even know who I am!!
MARY JANE:	You are Angel Cruz, you are thirty years old, you live with your mom on Tiemen Place, West Harlem. You have one felony prior, a robbery, you were sixteen. You work as a bike messenger. You had a year of college, you played soccer —
ANGEL:	I never played soccer.
MARY JANE:	You're charged with Attempted Murder, I know that.
ANGEL:	Attempted Murder??!!

```
MARY JANE:  — That surprises you? —
   ANGEL:  — Ya see bitch? Dass exactly what I'm
           talking 'bout. All I did —
MARY JANE:  — Stop!
   ANGEL:  All I did was shoot him in the ass, what
           the fuck is "attempted murder" about that,
           huh? . . . Stupid ass! . . . What??!!
(Mary Jane rises, begins collecting her things.)
           What are you doing?
MARY JANE:  I'm leaving.
   ANGEL:  Why, 'cuz I called you a bitch?
MARY JANE:  No, because you just confessed to me.
   ANGEL:  Confessed? Confessed what?
MARY JANE:  You just admitted to me that you did
           the shooting.
   ANGEL:  No I didn't!
MARY JANE:  You just said, "All I did was shoot him
           in the ass."
   ANGEL:  So?
MARY JANE:  So now you get your wish: I can't
           adequately defend you now, so you'll
           get another lawyer.
   ANGEL:  What if I don't want another lawyer?
MARY JANE:  You just got through haranguing me.
   ANGEL:  Haranguing?
MARY JANE:  It means —
   ANGEL:  I know what the hell it means.
```

The scene goes on with them getting more and more upset with each
other as Mary Jane says she can no longer represent him. The exchange ends with:

```
MARY JANE:  Lemme give you a little tip, Angel. The
            trick, Angel, is not to have a lawyer
            who makes no mistakes, but to get the
            lawyer who (A) makes the least mistakes
            and (B) is either green enough or
            masochistic enough to actually give a
            shit about their clients.
   ANGEL:   So which one are you?
MARY JANE:  I'm neither.
```

(Mary Jane exits. Blackout.)

Now that you know the ending, you may be even more tempted to make Mary Jane a nasty woman who is fed up with all her clients and has no other dimensions. You might be tempted to make Angel a hardened criminal who is abusive and mean. If you make these limited choices, then you have two unattractive, nasty people. Who wants to waste time with such people? Who wants to cast such people?

> ANGEL: — What I want is a fuckin' lawyer!! Is it possible, in this nightmare — I mean, what the fuck is this?! Even on TV they get a lawyer —

Angel's vulnerability should be obvious right away. Imagine yourself as a minority in a cruel white world. You made one small mistake and now you are in jail accused of attempted murder. You didn't intend to murder anyone. You are terrified and helpless and *on the verge of tears*. You have an incompetent lawyer who is a *woman*. You never met a woman lawyer before, and you don't trust them. If you bring all these aspects into these first lines the audience will sympathize and identify with you. There are many Fighting Fors you could use as Angel. He could be Fighting to prove he is tough. Or he could Fight to have Mary Jane save him. Your choice should allow for his vulnerability to show.

Don't rush his first speech and make everything sound the same. What word describes your feelings? The word *nightmare* should be searched for and thought up in the moment.

MARY JANE: I am a lawyer. I am your lawyer —

Instead of *just* giving information, Mary Jane should show compassion and understanding. She can smile with some humor. We should like her and sympathize with her, which we won't do if she looks exasperated. Mary Jane can be Fighting to be the best lawyer for Angel. At the end she makes a Mistake out of her frustration with him and gets angry, but for most of the scene she works hard to be good to him.

> ANGEL: I wanna real lawyer.

We should see Mary Jane receive the comment, digest it, and *then* answer with patience. She is intelligent enough to know he doesn't believe that a woman could be a "real lawyer."

```
MARY JANE:   I am a real lawyer and you are my real
             client. —
```

Make sure we see the two different concepts. Don't run the lines together. She can even point to herself and then to him if she does it with humor and a smile for him.

```
ANGEL:   Fuck that!
```

Mary Jane should receive this nasty comment with strength. We don't want a bitter *conversation* that goes back and forth and on and on. Mary Jane has to pause to gather herself so she doesn't scream back at him and then she has to think up a good idea to convince him. We must see the effort this takes her. Mary Jane could be Fighting to be the best lawyer she can be. But we see flashes of her despair and fury at dealing with so many people for whom she can do so little.

```
MARY JANE:   You wanna see the paperwork?
    ANGEL:   Fuck the paperwork! Why didn't you check
             the paperwork before you come in here
             talking all kinda shit when you didn't
             even know who you was speakin' to?
MARY JANE:   Look I am sorry for the mix-up, I —
```

Don't *just* apologize. Use subtext. Mary Jane could shake her head, give a small laugh at how awful this situation is, and apologize with humor and compassion. She really is sorry.

```
ANGEL:   The "mix-up"? Is that what happened
         before? Or do you just never know who
         anybody is?
```

Angel can now play a game. *Ohhhhh.* "Is *that* what happened before?" The word *mix-up* is a sarcastic game. The sarcasm gives him another dimension. It makes him feel superior for a moment. It feels good. He relishes it.

```
MARY JANE:   I'm sorry.
    ANGEL:   I ain't Hector Villanueva!!
```

Again Angel relishes his temporary superiority and his own humor.

```
MARY JANE:   I know that —
    ANGEL:   Hector Villanueva, NO Aqui!!
```

Angel has made a joke. He is proud of himself. He is winning the exchange briefly.

```
MARY JANE:   OK, what I need from you —
```

The exchange escalates. Mary Jane tries to get on top of the situation by raising her voice higher each time. She is not angry; she is trying to gain control so she can start working. Each exchange tops the other. It stops with "OK." *OK* should have finality to it. The subtext should be *let's stop this exchange*. Then Mary Jane becomes the professional when she says, "What I need from you —" These are two unrelated thoughts.

```
    ANGEL:   Need?! You gonna sit and talk to me
             about what you need? I'm incarcerated,
             lady! Why can't we talk about what I
             fuckin' need?!
```

Angel is not ready to get down to business. He still wants to use sarcasm to stay on top of the situation. The first *need* stands by itself. It is huge. The next line tops it. Make the line "You gonna sit and talk to me about what you need?" a huge mock Discovery, with the emphasis on *need*. Play big games here and show Angel's delight in getting Mary Jane's goat.

```
MARY JANE:   What do you need?
```

With this line Mary Jane stops trying to control the situation. We should see her deliberately taking another tack. She concedes to what Angel wants. *Okay, let's play it your way* is the subtext. (She is "starting the scene over.")

```
    ANGEL:   I need a damn lawyer!
```

Angel is at the height of frustration. His energy is way up. He can even appear dangerous.

```
MARY JANE:   Which is why I'm here —
```

Mary Jane is still patient and understanding and using some humor. We must like her. But her patience is slipping, so her tone might be sharper, with steel underneath.

> ANGEL: This is bullshit! This is racism is what
> it is, racism!! If I was white, I'd
> have a motherfuckin' Perry Mason sittin'
> here wit' the little glasses and the
> beard talking fuckin' strategy. Instead
> they give me some bumbling'-ass Wilma
> Flintstone don't even know who I am!!

Angel's speech is full of fury and hurt and frustration. There can be a hint of tears under the lines. Make sure you don't run all the lines together. Make sure the *little glasses* and the *beard* and the *bumbling* are all good images *for your partner.* You can put your hands up to your face to emphasize the glasses and the beard to Mary Jane. Take your time to create them.

> MARY JANE: You are Angel Cruz, you are thirty years
> old, you live with your mom on Tiemen
> Place, West Harlem. You have one felony
> prior, a robbery, you were sixteen. You
> work as a bike messenger. You had a
> year of college, you played soccer —

This is the third approach Mary Jane is taking to make Angel see reason. She is starting the scene over again by showing him she's done her homework. Now she is describing him from her notes. Make sure the items in the lists are distinguished from each other. Also, you have a wonderful opportunity as Mary Jane to give Angel a gift with the last two items. She makes a *Discovery* from her notes in this moment that he has gone to college. It flatters him that she is impressed. More surprising than his going to college is that he played soccer. She can think that is *great.* Now we like and appreciate Mary Jane and we don't see *just* a stern, boring lawyer.

> ANGEL: I never played soccer.

After all that she does know about him, he has to concentrate on the one thing she got wrong. Angel's reaction can be endearingly childish and petulant. It is a small and pathetic win. But he is impressed by her knowledge of his life.

```
MARY JANE:   You're charged with Attempted Murder, I
             know that.
```

Now Mary Jane's humor surfaces again. It is as if she is saying, "Okayyy, I got *that* wrong but I know *this*."

```
    ANGEL:   Attempted Murder??!!
```

This stops Angel dead in his tracks. Let the huge Discovery hit him before he says the line.

```
MARY JANE:   — That surprises you? —
```

Mary Jane also stops dead. Something is not right here. Remember, silences are what make a scene interesting. An average conversation between a lawyer and a client will not hold an audience's attention.

```
    ANGEL:   — Ya see bitch? Dass exactly what I'm
             talking 'bout. All I did —
MARY JANE:   — Stop!
```

Mary Jane wants to stop him from telling her he shot at someone.

```
    ANGEL:   All I did was shoot him in the ass, what
             the fuck is "attempted murder" about that,
             huh? . . . Stupid ass! . . . What??!!
```

Angel thinks he has some points to score on Mary Jane and nothing is going to stop him. Each line puts her down more and more. Use a game-playing sarcasm on "attempted murder." He gets big pleasure from feeling superior. Don't forget to differentiate each line from the other.

```
(Mary Jane rises, begins collecting her things.)
```

She should do this efficiently and professionally. (Remember: how you deal with your props reveals your state of mind.) She simply puts her papers back in her briefcase and rises. She is not letting Angel get to her, but on the other hand she is relieved she no longer has to deal with him.

    ANGEL: What are you doing?

We see Angel's confusion.

MARY JANE: I'm leaving.

She should say this coolly and matter-of-factly.

    ANGEL: Why, 'cuz I called you a bitch?

Angel is now scared and vulnerable again.

```
MARY JANE:  No, because you just confessed to me.
    ANGEL:  Confessed? Confessed what?
MARY JANE:  You just admitted to me that you did
            the shooting.
    ANGEL:  No I didn't!
```

His line tops Mary Jane's.

```
MARY JANE:  You just said, "All I did was shoot him
            in the ass."
```

She won. She got in the last word. There is pleasure in the small win.

    ANGEL: So?

His line is full of bravado even though underneath he is out of his depth and confused. We should feel for him the way we feel for a kid in the principal's office.

```
MARY JANE:  So now you get your wish: I can't
            adequately defend you now, so you'll
            get another lawyer.
```

Mary Jane can't help feeling the satisfaction of winning and of making the final point. We must see her pleasure in her win in the subtext, although on the surface she is professional.

    ANGEL: What if I don't want another lawyer?

Now Angel appears like the little boy he is inside. He admits he likes her and wants her to stay. As Angel, take your time before you say this line. You don't *want* to show such vulnerability. You *have* to. This line is a big event Beat and is in strong contrast to all of Angel's other lines, which are full of bluster and bravado.

MARY JANE: You just got through haranguing me.

Mary Jane is surprised by his admission. Very surprised. She takes time to make the Discovery that he is serious.

    ANGEL: Haranguing?
MARY JANE: It means —

Mary Jane doesn't need to feel superior now. She has won and it wouldn't be nice to rub it in.

    ANGEL: I know what the hell it means.

Angel takes back some of his power with this line, so it should be strong.

    The scene goes on with them getting more and more upset with each other as Mary Jane says she can no longer represent him. The exchange ends with:

MARY JANE: Lemme give you a little tip, Angel. The
               trick, Angel, is not to have a lawyer
               who makes no mistakes but to get the
               lawyer who (A) makes the least mistakes
               and (B) is either green enough or
               masochistic enough to actually give a
               shit about their clients.
    ANGEL: So which one are you?
MARY JANE: I'm neither.

Angel loses. Big time. We should see him realizing it and his acceptance of his defeat.

    Mary Jane has the win she wants. She was patient. She was professional. She was compassionate. Nothing worked and now she wants to punish him. Her frustration and resentment and her history with difficult clients surfaces. She tells him she's not only a lawyer who makes mistakes, but also a lawyer who doesn't "give a shit" about her clients. But don't let this last speech color all your work as Mary Jane. By the time she gets to this angry place, you, as the actress, have shown many dimensions and you didn't fall into the trap of being a one-note, fed-up lawyer. Mary Jane should take a Beat to think what kind of a lawyer she is and *then* she says, "I'm neither."

> **TIP**: *Don't play the ending from the beginning.*

If you know you are going to lose in the end, don't let that color your work. If you know you are going to kick out your lover in the end, don't let that stop you from trying to change the qualities you don't like so you don't have to kick him/her out.

Angel has shown not just anger but vulnerability, pleasure in scoring points, game-playing (sarcasm), and finally defeat.

If you play the parts with all these dimensions, you will be likable and will not get trapped in the clichés of an angry lawyer and a nasty criminal. We will like, understand, and feel for both of you.

The Trap of Typecasting Your Own Character

The following scene from *The Prettiest Girl*, by Ashley Leahy, is also full of traps. If you fall into them you will appear unattractive in the roles. The characters are at a cocktail party.

ANGIE: You are beautiful. Everyone in the room is looking at you. Not because they see you as strange, but because you are the prettiest girl in the room.

FRANK: Excuse me, but could you put down the deviled eggs? The other guests might want to partake.

ANGIE: This man wants your advice on the universe. Look at how his left eyebrow is raised in disbelief. He cannot fathom how anyone could be so stunning. (*To Frank*) Yes I will help you.

FRANK: Help me by giving me that tray.

ANGIE: You're smiling at me.

FRANK: No, I'm looking past you.

ANGIE: It's all right, no need to be afraid. (*She takes hold of his arm.*) You can touch my face. (*She places his hand on her cheek.*) Was it good for you?

FRANK: How long have you been a patient here?

ANGIE: (*Picking up a deviled egg and stuffing it into her mouth.*) I can't taste a thing.

FRANK: How many of those have you eaten?

ANGIE: Take two capsules daily on a full stomach.

FRANK: All right, eat the whole damn plate. See if I care. (*He turns to go.*)

ANGIE: He's leaving you. Not a good sign. (*To Frank.*) Wait.

FRANK: Why?

ANGIE: I just remembered where I know you from.

FRANK: Okay . . .

ANGIE: Halloween.

FRANK: I wasn't here on Halloween. (*He starts to leave.*)

ANGIE: Nor was I.

FRANK: Then what . . .

ANGIE: The movie. I was watching the movie *Halloween*, and I saw you. You walked into the theatre with a blonde lady. She looked like my sister. I remembered you because she looked like my sister.

FRANK: (*Trying to remember.*) I don't think . . .

ANGIE: Don't tell him what you did next. He'll forget you're beautiful. (*To Frank.*) It was you. You drove a green convertible.

FRANK: (*Remembers.*) I remember that day now. A girl was screaming and crying. It was my first date with Paula.

ANGIE: First dates are always magical.

FRANK: She was sitting a few rows behind us. I remember thinking it odd that she would scream and shout before the movie even began.

(*Angie grows agitated, stuffs two more deviled eggs into her mouth.*)

FRANK: And then we saw the blood. A lot of blood and screaming and no one was even watching

> the movie anymore. They were all looking at
> her. They were all staring at her with her
> bloody arms and her crazy eyes because . . .
>
> ANGIE: Because she was the prettiest girl in the
> room.

Suppose you have an audition and (although you asked) you received no information except that these are two characters at a cocktail party. What choices do you make? If you fall into the trap that Angie is nuts and talks a lot about nothing and that Frank sees she is nuts and is Fighting to get away from her, you have not done your homework.

> ANGIE: You are beautiful. Everyone in the room is
> looking at you. Not because they see you as
> strange, but because you are the prettiest
> girl in the room.

Don't say these lines in a relaxed manner as if you are giving yourself a mild pep talk. Risk! Go far. Say them as if you are falling apart. As though you are terrified. Use energy. Each line is separated and distinct from the others, and each line is important in a different way.

> FRANK: Excuse me, but could you put down the deviled
> eggs? The other guests might want to partake.

This line sounds nasty. But is it? Look at the word *partake*. Isn't it an unusual word to use in this situation? Couldn't he be playing a game with her? Couldn't he be flirting? Wouldn't that choice be more fun and make him seem more attractive? Choose that she is stunning and he is attracted to her.

> ANGIE: This man wants your advice on the universe.
> Look at how his left eyebrow is raised in
> disbelief. He cannot fathom how anyone
> could be so stunning. (*To Frank*) Yes I will
> help you.

Angie could look away to say the first three lines to herself, or she could look at him for all of the lines and Frank could be fascinated, thinking she is playing a game he doesn't understand. Make sure Angie makes a delightful Discovery about his eyebrow, and that she sneaks a look at the eyebrow before she says the line. Then she turns and says the line to Frank in a completely different tone. "Yes," she could say ecstatically, "I will help you." After all, she is not helping him with merely the deviled eggs, she is helping him with advice on the universe.

FRANK: Help me by giving me that tray.

Frank is still intrigued. This line *must not be said straight*; it must be said flirtatiously.

ANGIE: You're smiling at me.

This line should be said not merely as a fact, but with amazement as a major Discovery. She is thrilled. Most people walk away from her, because she makes them nervous.

FRANK: No, I'm looking past you.

Don't say this straight. Say it teasingly.

ANGIE: It's all right, no need to be afraid. (*She takes hold of his arm.*) You can touch my face. (*She places his hand on her cheek.*) Was it good for you?

Don't do these lines too fast. Taking hold of his arm is an event for both of them. He is attracted and intrigued. After a moment, when he puts his hand on her face, we should wonder if they are going to kiss. The attraction is strong. When she asks if it was good for him, she should be serious. He senses her inappropriate reaction, but if it makes him pull away and dismiss her, we don't have an interesting scene. Frank is attracted and curious and he wants to understand her. The audience should also sense a mystery. The audience should laugh at the line "Was it good for you?" because it is usually said only after sex.

FRANK: How long have you been a patient here?

He does know something is off, but this should be said with laughter. He is teasing her, but he also wants reassurance she is not crazy.

ANGIE: (*Picking up a deviled egg and stuffing it into her mouth.*) I can't taste a thing.

When my students did this scene, they all picked up the eggs too fast. Let Angie *receive* Frank's line with a Beat. Let her panic that Frank has discovered she is insane. *Then* she uses the eggs for comfort. *Then* she panics that she can't taste the eggs. Each one should be a separate step. They can happen quickly, one after another, but they should be distinct.

FRANK: How many of those have you eaten?

Don't say this line straight, as if all you want is information. Ask with concern.

ANGIE: Take two capsules daily on a full stomach.

The words act as a talisman to keep her from flying apart. Go far with how out of control she is. She can barely hold it together. Her body is tense. Frank senses something is off but he is still ready to believe she is just playing.

FRANK: All right, eat the whole damn plate. See if I care. (*He turns to go.*)

This line is a trap waiting to suck you in. Don't say it with indifference, as if you don't give a damn (the worst actor choice). Say it with a game. *All right* could be said with an up-tilt at the end. *All ri-ight.* Use humor. Threaten to leave, but don't really mean it. Frank must want to get to the bottom of this mystery. He wants to be called back. Remember how beautiful Angie is.

ANGIE: He's leaving you. Not a good sign. (*To Frank.*) Wait.

"Wait" is said with urgency.

FRANK: Why?

Don't *just* ask a question. He asks "Why?" because he wants her to convince him that she finds him valuable. He thinks he will get a compliment.

```
ANGIE:   I just remembered where I know you from.
FRANK:   Okay . . .
```

He draws out the line. He wants to be convinced to stay.

```
ANGIE:   Halloween.
FRANK:   I wasn't here on Halloween. (He starts to
         leave.)
```

Stage directions in any play should almost invariably be ignored. If Frank starts to leave without looking back, he has fallen into the trap of indifference and we don't have a scene. If he leaves hoping to be called back, we enjoy the scene.

> **TIP:** *Ignore stage directions if they are not helpful. Often they were written in by the stage manager and relate only to the first production. Stage directions often tell you to sigh or look weary or indifferent— all terrible actor choices.*

```
ANGIE:   Nor was I.
FRANK:   Then what . . .
```

Choose that Frank really wants to know where they could have met before. Maybe her mystery will clear up then.

```
ANGIE:   The movie. I was watching the movie
         Halloween, and I saw you. You walked into
         the theatre with a blonde lady. She looked
         like my sister. I remembered you because she
         looked like my sister.
```

Don't *just* play the lines straight about the sister. Make an interesting choice for how important the sister is. Perhaps Angie was ripped apart from her sister in a custody battle when she was very young. Perhaps her sister is in jail, and thinking she saw her sister in the movies stunned Angie. There should be intensity in Angie's talk about her sister that worries Frank.

```
FRANK:   (Trying to remember.) I don't think . . .
ANGIE:   Don't tell him what you did next. He'll
         forget you're beautiful. (To Frank.) It was
         you. You drove a green convertible.
FRANK:   (Remembers.) I remember that day now. A girl
         was screaming and crying. It was my first
         date with Paula.
```

Frank makes a big Discovery. As he remembers the girl screaming, it dawns on him that the girl might be Angie. Remember, an actor understands information as quickly as does the audience. We suspect the screamer was Angie, so he should too. Also remember that most people are good liars, so don't make it obvious that Frank knows. He hides it from Angie.

ANGIE: First dates are always magical.

This line also is not said straight, but with conviction and intensity to distract Frank from the truth that she was the screamer. Search for the word *magical*. Sift through other choices before you find it.

FRANK: She was sitting a few rows behind us. I
         remember thinking it odd that she would
         scream and shout before the movie even began.

Frank gives Angie the message that he suspects she was the girl, and he wants her to confirm it.

(*Angie grows agitated, stuffs two more deviled eggs
into her mouth.*)

Angie has to receive the event that Frank knows with a Beat. *Then* she eats the eggs to comfort herself.

FRANK: And then we saw the blood. A lot of blood
         and screaming and no one was even watching
         the movie anymore. They were all looking at
         her. They were all staring at her with her
         bloody arms and her crazy eyes because . . .

With *because* Frank interrupts himself. He is probably going to say it was the weirdest thing he ever saw and they all knew the girl was crazy. With each line Frank is more and more sure Angie was the girl. Keep the images in his speech strong. We should see the girl with blood all over her, screaming. If you are playing Frank don't *just* give information. With each line he accumulates more certainty that Angie was the crazy girl—and he gives Angie the message of that certainty.

ANGIE: Because she was the prettiest girl in the
         room.

This line must burst forth from Angie with desperation and terror. She needs to cover up to Frank that she was the girl. She needs to assure him and herself that everyone was staring at the girl because she was pretty and not because she was covered in blood and acting crazy. Risk! The word room is the highest in pitch of all the words in that sentence because of her terror.

Angie is the crazy girl and Frank has no idea which way to jump now. It is scary for him. What should he do or say? At the end of the scene they hold a Beat, which acknowledges they both have the same information. The last moment is full of tension. What next?

What was Angie Fighting For? Perhaps to make Frank fall in love with her. The stakes are high because most men walk away from her. Maybe Frank is her last chance for happiness. She sees him as her ideal man. She falls in love instantly.

Frank could be Fighting to be perfect for Angie. At first he tries to impress her with his games and flirting and then he tries to be perfect so she will not fall apart on him. Being perfect is hard work. Angie keeps Frank on his toes at all times.

How to Make a Genre Scene Look Like Shakespeare

The following scene is from a thriller called *Snake Charmer*, based on a novel by John Griffiths, adapted by Gerry Daly, Marc Springer, and me, with a screenplay by Gerry Daly.

A student in a boarding school, Lisa, has fallen or been pushed off a cliff. The teacher, Nolan, doesn't want to believe she was murdered because the scandal could cause the school to fold. The cop, Jacobson, who was trained by his Native American boss, has analyzed tracks and believes she was pushed. In order to get Nolan to help him, Jacobson has taken him rock climbing and arranged that he should fall to experience what Lisa went through. Of course Nolan was held by a rope and is fine, but he is still having an adrenaline rush from his recent tumble.

```
EXT — TOP OF THE CLIFF — DAY

                    JACOBSON
     Now this is what makes the climb worthwhile.
```

                    NOLAN
That and experiencing your whole life
pass before you.

                    JACOBSON
What haunts me is what Lisa must have felt.

                    NOLAN
Felt?

                    JACOBSON
When she was falling, I mean. It always
scares me to death. But then it's not
the same as knowing there's a rope and
somebody reliable at the other end, is it?
          (Nolan suddenly tenses)
There's that split second of panic, then
you know you're okay. But how did she feel,
knowing her life had run out, forever?

                    NOLAN
You bastard. You sneaky manipulative
bastard. You planned this didn't you? You
knew I was going to fall and you let me.
You scared the shit out of me, endangered
my life, just to make some kind of point?

                    JACOBSON
I checked the rope very thoroughly.

                    NOLAN
I could have been killed.

                    JACOBSON
Lisa *was* killed. Murdered. Deliberately
and coldly. And if you don't help me, her
killer will get away with it. Is that
what you want?

This is the kind of scene you will often be asked to play. How do you
make it transcend the genre and rivet the audience? By making it a
contest between two equally strong men. Each one wants something

from the other. Jacobson's Fighting For is obvious. He wants Nolan to help him solve the murder and he is using every means he can think of to achieve this end.

Nolan's Fighting For is less obvious. He must be intelligent enough to know that Jacobson wants something. (Remember, actors should understand information as soon as the audience does.) In the lines shown here, Nolan is Fighting to punish Jacobson for letting him fall.

Look at each actor's first lines. Make them actions, not just chat.

> JACOBSON
> Now this is what makes the climb worthwhile.

> NOLAN
> That and experiencing your whole life
> pass before you.

The intention of Jacobson's line could be to set Nolan at ease and establish a friendly atmosphere before he makes his point.

Nolan's first line could be to prove he was not freaked out by his fall. He should use humor and even laugh at the experience. Jacobson admires Nolan's courage with a smile. Then he gets down to business.

> JACOBSON
> What haunts me is what Lisa must have felt.

> NOLAN
> Felt?

Nolan immediately (and intelligently) begins to understand that Jacobson has an agenda. Nolan should pause before this line. He is figuring it out. The worst actor choice would be for him not to have heard correctly or be completely clueless about Jacobson's meaning.

> JACOBSON
> When she was falling, I mean. It always
> scares me to death. But then it's not
> the same as knowing there's a rope and
> somebody reliable at the other end, is it?

Jacobson is giving Nolan a very specific message. Jacobson can laugh on "It always scares me to death," but then he gets serious. Don't forget "is it?" at the end. Expect an answer to all questions, and wait for it here in order to add tension and communication, instead of making the words just an add-on.

```
               (Nolan suddenly tenses)
```

Nolan tenses because he makes the huge Discovery that Jacobson let him fall on purpose. He should barely be able to restrain himself from punching Jacobson. His body should reflect his fury. At the very least, he has to change position. Don't indicate in a fake manner for the audience that you have finally understood. You want *Jacobson* to know you are on to his scheme.

```
There's that split second of panic, then
you know you're okay. But how did she feel,
knowing her life had run out, forever?
```

Jacobson knows that Nolan is furious. He continues anyway. Make sure that the phrase "her life had run out" is separated from "forever." They should be equal in importance.

```
                    NOLAN
You bastard. You sneaky manipulative
bastard. You planned this didn't you? You
knew I was going to fall and you let me.
You scared the shit out of me, endangered
my life, just to make some kind of point?
```

Nolan should really let fly now. The more you risk as Nolan with expressing your anger, the more compelling you will be. With each line Nolan is more sure of what Jacobson did to him. Maybe Nolan gets up. He shouts. He makes Discoveries as he goes along. Separate "you knew I was going to fall" from "and you let me." The last phrase should be so unbelievable to Nolan that it rises in pitch. "You scared the shit out of me" is equally important, so make it very clear to Jacobson. "Endangered my life" rises in importance over the previous phrase, followed by "just to make some kind of *point*?" Each line rises in importance over the last one. Nolan is shaking with anger. Don't be just a little upset. This man risked your *life*.

```
                  JACOBSON
I checked the rope very thoroughly.
```

Let Jacobson pause before this line. He acknowledges Nolan's point first. Then he gives an excuse. It should contain some wry humor.

```
                    NOLAN
    I could have been killed.
```

Nolan calms slightly so he can give Jacobson a specific message about how wrong he was. He says this line as a fact. He makes it a strong event/Beat.

```
                    JACOBSON
    Lisa was killed. Murdered. Deliberately
    and coldly. And if you don't help me, her
    killer will get away with it. Is that
    what you want?
```

If, as Jacobson, you immediately answer Nolan, then you have lost power. Jacobson should look at Nolan first. Note the emphasis on "was." Use it. Say "Lisa *was* killed." Then pause again. This line is the biggest event of the scene. Make each word—*murdered, deliberately, coldly*—have its own weight and power. Each is different. Jacobson is working hard. His final question is asked with a demand for an answer. He waits for that answer. They hold the silence.

This final silent moment has subtext. Jacobson is challenging Nolan, and Nolan looks back at him ready to answer. By this time Nolan will have accepted that he has to help. The moment contains that admission. They hold the charged look until the director says "Cut."

If the actors achieve all of this, they will have a powerful scene.

There should always be subtext and needs and conflict between characters. Never *just* chat. Look at the following scene from the same screenplay between the teacher, Nolan, and the headmaster of the school, Ewing Sinclair. They are discussing the death of the student who fell off a cliff.

```
INT — SINCLAIR'S OFFICE — DAY

Sinclair and Nolan are in the office.

                    SINCLAIR
    You mean they just let her go off? She's
    stoned, possibly hallucinating and they
```

let her go off . . . Alone . . . In the
pitch dark?

                    NOLAN
Robert thought she was all right. It
never occurred to them to worry.

                    SINCLAIR
Never occurred to them? Nothing ever
occurs to them except the gratification
of the moment. Did they hear anything?
Did they hear her scream?

                    NOLAN
Maybe it was too windy, or . . .

                    SINCLAIR
Or what?

                    NOLAN
She wouldn't scream if she thought she
could fly.

Both men quietly stare at each other.

                    SINCLAIR
Would it show up in the autopsy? I mean
if you weren't looking for it . . .

                    NOLAN
It's evidence, Ewing. If you think it's
bad now, think how it will look if they
find us withholding evidence.

Sinclair faintly smiles.

                    SINCLAIR
I'll have a word with the sheriff. You
think I'm unfeeling, don't you?

                    NOLAN
I think you have a healthy regard for the
practical.

                    SINCLAIR
    Perhaps too healthy a regard?

                    NOLAN
    Perhaps.

                    SINCLAIR
    We're a small school. We can't afford
    scandal. So I'll be doing my damnedest to
    head this one off. Even at the cost of
    appearing . . . (he gives Nolan a rueful
    smile) too ruthlessly practical.

If you let them merely chat about this death and what to do about it, there is no tension or stakes in the scene. Raise the stakes to a war of morals between two intelligent men.

Sinclair is Fighting For Nolan to think well of him no matter how far he may go to save the school from scandal.

Nolan is Fighting For Sinclair to do the correct thing.

Look at the first lines.

                    SINCLAIR
    You mean they just let her go off? She's
    stoned, possibly hallucinating and they
    let her go off . . . Alone . . . In the
    pitch dark?

                    NOLAN
    Robert thought she was all right. It
    never occurred to them to worry.

The Fighting For of Sinclair's first line is to blame Nolan. If he can put Nolan on the defensive, then Nolan might listen to him and let him have his way. Each line after that should set the scene for Nolan, make him see the image of the girl. "She's stoned," also "possibly hallucinating." And "they let her go off," "alone," and finally the worst yet, "in the pitch dark?" He is outraged.

The action of Nolan's first line is to defend Robert's action. Nolan's first line doesn't convince Sinclair, so after a brief pause Nolan adds another thought. "It never occurred to them to worry."

> SINCLAIR
> Never occurred to them? Nothing ever
> occurs to them except the gratification
> of the moment. Did they hear anything?

Sinclair's first line in this speech is a question. He should ask and then expect an answer for a few seconds before he continues. There should be no rhetorical questions in acting. Pause to wait for the answer. Then when it is not forthcoming, move on. Note the rising frustration in the speech.

> SINCLAIR
> Did they hear her scream?

> NOLAN
> Maybe it was too windy, or . . .

This is the biggest Beat or event in the scene. Nolan is about to say that Lisa might have been high. If she fell because she was high, the school is in big trouble. Parents might pull their kids out and the school could close. There should be a long pause after Nolan's line. Sinclair doesn't want to know any more bad news at first. Then his curiosity gets the better of him and he reluctantly asks:

> SINCLAIR
> Or what?

Nolan takes his time to say the next line. He knows it is a bomb. Sinclair dares him to say what he knows.

> NOLAN
> She wouldn't scream if she thought she
> could fly.

Sinclair must receive this huge event with another Beat. The two men look at each other as they absorb the import of her having possibly taken hallucinatory drugs. Risk by prolonging the silence. It will be powerful to the audience.

> SINCLAIR
> Would it show up in the autopsy? I mean
> if you weren't looking for it . . .

Sinclair's suggestion of hiding the evidence is unethical. Use his intelligence. He is not asking a question of fact only. He knows it, and Nolan knows it. The subtext is important. Use your own sense of right and wrong. Maybe in this case Sinclair thinks the ends justify the means. He is torn. This is not easy for him to say. Nolan should not reply right away. He has to acknowledge Sinclair's moral dilemma. Then Nolan gently rebukes Sinclair.

```
                    NOLAN
     It's evidence, Ewing. If you think it's
     bad now, think how it will look if they
     find us withholding evidence.
```

Nolan should find some humor in these lines.

```
Sinclair smiles faintly.
```

These two men are both intelligent. They know that the subtext is a discussion of values and that Ewing wants to fudge his ethics. The actors must know it too.

```
                    SINCLAIR
     I'll have a word with the sheriff. You
     think I'm unfeeling, don't you?
```

Sinclair gives in and says he will do the right thing and tell the sheriff their suspicions. After he agrees, he has a completely different thought. He wants to know what Nolan thinks of him. Make sure there is a pause between the two sentences.

```
                    NOLAN
     I think you have a healthy regard for the
     practical.
```

This line should also have some humor in it. Nolan is letting Sinclair off the hook by saying he knows that Sinclair's momentary ethical lapse was caused by his concern for the school.

```
                    SINCLAIR
     Perhaps too healthy a regard?

                    NOLAN
     Perhaps.
```

Both Nolan's and Sinclair's lines should have humor in them. Nolan can smile on "Perhaps." We should see their friendship and respect for each other. Then Sinclair rationalizes his moral lapse.

```
                    SINCLAIR
        We're a small school. We can't afford
        scandal. So I'll be doing my damnedest to
        head this one off. Even at the cost of
        appearing . . . (he gives Nolan a rueful
        smile) too ruthlessly practical.
```

If this scene is done using subtext, events, silences, and humor, it will transcend the action genre and make the actors look brilliant. Actors who can make scenes like this riveting are never out of work.

Summary

Every scene you do should be analyzed carefully for subtext, under-currents, needs, and wants. Never be satisfied to say the lines as written. Don't play them straight. Always look for ways to add your own reactions and your vulnerability. If your character is angry, don't be satisfied with shouting at your partner. Access the pain that causes your anger. If the scene is with your mother, use all the complications of your relationship with your own mother. (You will never have a more complicated relationship). Never leave out humor, even if it is just a small exhalation of amused disbelief at your partner's point of view. Have a strong Fighting For and raise the stakes of every scene.

9 Technique

Talent Is Not Enough

Acting is a craft and there are techniques to master. Even if your talent is outstanding, you won't have a career if you don't have a strong technique.

An excellent technique is a safety net that doesn't let you fall below a certain level. You may not do your best work each performance, but with a good technique you'll never be less than professional. Technique is learned and must be practiced. You cannot just *wing* a performance and expect to be marvelous. Occasionally winging it may work, but more often it will not. Casting directors don't bring back actors who blew it even once, because you embarrassed them in front of their employers—the producers and director.

A strong technique frees you creatively. You can't do your best work if you are worrying about where you are standing or if your hair is in your eyes. You can't do your best audition if you're wondering how to hold the script. Part of a good technique is knowing how to handle yourself on a set or a stage.

Your Voice

Don't let yourself get away with an unnaturally low volume because you think that you are acting in front of a camera and you want to be "real." Instead you will be boring and not real at all. In my class I speak with energy because I care enough about my students to want to get my point across. You must care about your partner enough to use your full voice. If you need to whisper, use intensity to make up for your quietness.

Actors and even directors may think the hushed quality of breathiness also makes performances more intense and "real." The truth is, however, if you aren't using your natural volume, you're not committing sufficiently to your Fighting For. Breathiness quickly becomes irritating.

Some directors allow or even encourage breathiness. A good example is *Neverland*. You may have enjoyed the film, but look at it again and see if you don't agree that the actors should have used their real voices. I found the breathiness annoying. Look at *Kite Runner*. Many of the scenes could have been more dramatic, riveting, and moving if the actors had been directed to use their full voices and full energy.

Many women get shrill when they are angry or excited, and shrillness can be more irritating than breathiness. Ask someone to check your pitch. No matter what I said to one girl in my class, she always became shrill when the stakes of the scene rose. One day I told her she came across as girly, and suggested she try to be more womanly. From then on, not only did her voice sound better, but her work increased in power. Her partners now had to take her seriously.

Breath Control

I joke to my students that commercials and Shakespeare need the most breath control. Yet lines in between those extremes should never be interrupted by sloppy breath control.

Look at this speech from Shakespeare's *Twelfth Night*. It is the beginning of the play. The Duke is asking Valentine for news of the woman he has fallen in love with—Olivia. Valentine answers:

> So please my lord, I might not be admitted;
> But from her handmaid do return this answer:
> The element [sky] itself, till seven years' heat,

> Shall not behold her face at ample view;
> But, like a cloisteress, she will veiled walk,
> And water once a day her chamber round
> With eye-offending brine: all this to season
> A brother's dead love, which she would keep fresh
> And lasting in her sad remembrance.

Now read the speech again, noting the only places you are allowed to breathe without messing up the poetry or the sense of the lines.

> So please my lord, I might not be admitted;
> But from her handmaid do return this answer: (Breathe)
> The element [sky] itself, till seven years heat,
> Shall not behold her face at ample view; (Breathe)
> But, like a cloisteress, she will veiled walk, (Do not breathe here,
>   because walk and water must follow each other closely)
> And water once a day her chamber round
> With eye-offending brine: (Breathe) all this to season
> A brother's dead love, which she would keep fresh
> And lasting in her sad remembrance. (Breathe)

Now look at this commercial.

> Brine soap is made from the purest ingredients taken from the sea and made into a cleansing bar for your individualized type of skin. (Breathe) If you use this soap you will notice a softness, a shininess, and glow you have never seen before. (Breathe)

Don't breathe except between the two lines. Remember, commercials are written by committees and every word has cost thousands of dollars to research. Make each word worth the gold it cost.

When you breathe properly, you use more energy, so your voice becomes richer and has more depth.

How to Cry and How to Laugh

In my class I teach a technique of laughing and crying so that my actors can be confident of being able to repeat it when their inspiration dries up after ten takes. I can't count the number of times my students have called to tell me these techniques had "saved" them on a set.

Laughing is easy . . . at first. But sometimes you dry up. You feel strangled for air if you are asked to laugh on and on, or you feel fake and unfunny.

You may feel obliged to come up with real tears each time you repeat a scene. This can be impossible. You need a good technique as a safety net.

Laughing Out Loud—The Technique

Think of laughing as strong exhalations: Hah Hah Hah. The air is expelled outward in short bursts. The remedy for drying up and feeling strangled for air is to *feed the laughs* with air. Take a breath before you dry up. Take lots of inward breaths and exhale them out.

Practice laughing in front of the mirror. See what looks funny. See if you look natural. Learn to laugh without motivation at the drop of a hat. Learn to feed your laughs with inhalations. Women should take care not to sound shrill.

When I do the laughing exercise in class I have one actor laugh at a time. But if I look around the room all the other students are grinning too. Laughing is infectious even if it isn't motivated by something funny. Learn the technique of laughing and you will be funnier, and your laughter will be more natural because you won't be worried about faking or drying up.

Most laughter is not laugh-out-loud laughter. Small laughs cover embarrassment. Social laughs mask discomfort. Laughs can release tension, or express polite disbelief. The more laughs you put into your work, the fuller it is. Look for how and why people laugh in real life. You will be amazed how seldom laughs have to do with something comedic.

Crying—The Technique

The most important thing is to free yourself from the obligation of producing real tears. For most actors it is not possible to cry real tears time after time, re-take after re-take. If there is a close-up and if the director needs real tears, you can use glycerin or other such methods. (Ask in advance to have it on the set.) You can look as if you are crying even if tears are not pouring down your cheeks. On the stage you don't need real tears if you cry convincingly.

> **CRYING TIP 1:** *Don't cry generally. Each sob or tear is a reaction to a new thought or new information.*

Crying uses the opposite breathing of laughing. The air is brought *inward* as if you are trying not to cry. Try it now. You will almost feel as if you are sniffling. Then find the place on your face that you cry with. For example, when I cry my mouth turns down. Some people feel their eyes crinkling or their mouths tightening.

Now cry as if you are at a funeral. You are devastated but you shouldn't cry out loud because people will look at you. Look in the mirror and see what looks right. Get the technique down. You don't have to feel anything while you do this. Ask a friend to do this exercise with you. You will both be amazed at how realistic this "dry crying" looks.

Sobs can use the laughing exhalation technique. Don't squeak. Do the sobs with a lower register. Again, you are not obligated to feel anything. Just do the technique of crying in the mirror until you are confident that it looks natural. Of course it is better if you can produce real tears. Some actors are more gifted at this than others.

Some actors use the technique of working so hard *not* to cry that they look as though they are crying.

The great thing about being able to laugh and cry at will is that once you add the context of the scene, your technical tears and laughter can miraculously become real to you. Your fake tears can become real tears just as your fake laughs can become real laughs. This is because mastering the technique has taken away the stress and worry of appearing real.

CRYING TIP 2: If you want to think of something to make you cry real tears, I suggest you think of a new sad circumstance. Think of your best friend in a plane crash. Or think of your brother disappearing. Don't think about the death of someone who has already died, because you've processed that death. I say to my students, "Kill a fresh person." (On the other hand, some actors have been taught an Affective Memory exercise, which means you access an old sad memory to start your tears. Use what works for you.)

CRYING TIP 3: If you cry full out the audience will feel sorry for you. If you hold back your tears, the audience will tear up to make up for your bravery.

CRYING TIP 4: Do not cover your face. In life we are embarrassed by crying and we turn away or cover our faces with our hands. But actors need to show their faces. In my class I tell my students I want to see "naked faces." (Don't cover your mouth when you laugh either.)

> *CRYING TIP 5: Wipe away your real tears, as we do in life. Don't be so thrilled about achieving real tears that you let them pour down your cheeks as if you are proud of them.*

Make Your Tears Specific

I saw an actress do a comedy in which her partner was breaking up with her. The partner had lots of lines but the actress only cried and sobbed. What a hard part—and yet she was hilarious. The trap of the scene was that the crying could be a Molasses poured over the whole thing, producing an un-funny sameness. This actress, however, was so specific with her sobs and her reactions that she had the audience in stitches. Each time the partner said something new, the actress reacted. When she was really upset at some new information, she threw herself on the bed. When she heard the partner had been unfaithful, she jerked and sobbed even louder. In the end, as the partner was leaving, she howled. The audience too was howling, with laughter, because each sob was so specifically a *reaction* to a particular Discovery or event.

Technique for Cold Readings, aka Auditions

There is a misconception that cold readings are really cold, that you have never seen the script before and you plunge in not knowing the story. *Never* read a script for a casting director if you have not studied it up, down, and sideways. If you were not able to get the script before you arrived at the audition, take your time to prepare while other people audition ahead of you. Don't let anyone rush you.

There are many rules for cold readings. You must follow each of them.

1. Hold the script in one hand, slightly out from your body, and *leave it there*. I call it "floating the script." Don't let it flap up and down, hitting your leg each time you finish a line, or the auditor's attention will be on the script and not on you. If you don't move the script, it will become invisible to the auditors. Don't put the script down on a table or on your lap, or your attention will be directed downward and not at your partner.

2. Even if you have memorized your lines, hold the script anyway and refer to it now and then. If you don't glance at it, the auditors will

expect even more from your performance. Also, you might lose the lines if you are nervous and you should have the security of knowing they are close by.

3. If you are sitting during the audition, don't let either of your arms rest on your legs when you are reading. I have noticed that men, especially, allow their arms to rest on their legs and they remain glued there for the rest of the scene. Your stomach muscles won't be tight if you are hunched over yourself. You will lose energy. Watch it. Float the script!

4. Don't let your arm rest on the back of a chair or a couch. Once you start your performance it will feel impossible to unglue your arm from the furniture. Anyway, you should be Fighting so hard for what you want that you won't be resting any part of yourself.

5. If you have the choice of sitting or standing, always stand. You'll have more freedom to move around, and more energy. If you're doing a scene in a restaurant you have to sit, but do it as if you are being goosed. Don't slouch into your seat unless you are doing it on purpose to make a point. Sit up with energy.

6. Don't try to find your lines while your partner is speaking. Pay the utmost attention to your partner or the reader. If you ask your partner a question, don't look at your script before your partner has finished answering you. Never say your lines to the page. You have to learn to scoop up the words from the paper instantly, and you have to keep your place so you don't have to hunt for it. Some actors swear by the moving thumb method. They slide their thumbs down the script as they read. Also, use a highlighter to mark your lines. When students come to my class without a perfect reading technique, I tell them to practice reading in front of the mirror. Read anything out loud without expression and see how often and for how long you can meet your own eyes. Ten minutes twice a day for two weeks should make you a proficient reader. This technique must become second nature. Until you get it down perfectly, you are not free to give your attention to changing your partner.

7. Make sure when you are finding your lines you don't lose your energy. If you are shouting, "I hate you," don't lose that intensity while

you are finding your next line. Find your place in the script with the energy of your emotion.

8. If you lose your place never apologize, and *never* comment on it with a grimace. Never say "sorry." Find your place again in character and go on. It will seem like an eternity to you and just a few seconds to the auditor. *No one cares if you lose your place.* It will not affect the outcome. Probably no one will notice. Everyone will be annoyed if you *show* you lost your place. I had a friend who was auditioning for Mike Nichols. My friend dropped his script and pages floated all over the floor. He picked them up in character. Can you imagine how much the auditors admired him?

9. Never ask to start over. It is annoying to the auditors. In all the auditions I have attended many actors asked to start over, but not one was different the second time. Not one. Starting over is unprofessional. It means you weren't prepared. If you flub the first few lines, forge ahead.

10. If you are lucky enough to be reading with another actor (not just a reader) and you have to hug, don't try to read over your partner's shoulder. It is awkward and takes the auditors out of the scene. Hug or kiss and then back away to read your next line.

11. If you are being upstaged by another actor, move naturally away to rescue yourself. Walk upstage and get on the same parallel line (from stage left to stage right) as the other actor, so you are not turning your back on the audience. The ability to rescue yourself from being upstaged is second nature to seasoned actors.

12. Keep your hair out of your eyes with a bobby pin if necessary. There is nothing more distracting to an auditor than not being able to see an actor because of his or her hair. If your carefully pinned back hair comes undone and falls in your face, brush it away in character with the emotion of the scene. I have seen too many actors brush their hair away gently when they are furious with their partner in the scene.

13. It is important you stand with your body turned three-quarters to the auditors. Even if you are auditioning for film or television in a small office, you need to look professional. You have to know how to cheat forward so your audience can see you. You'd be amazed by the professional actors who hide themselves.

14. If you are doing a taped audition, don't look directly into the camera. Look as if you were talking to someone about five inches from the side of the lens.

15. When you enter the room to audition for a film or a stage audition, chat briefly and *start*. (Keep the greetings brief. Remember, they want to get home.)

Too many actors indulge in "taking a moment." They turn their backs to the auditors, breathe deeply, and give a huge sigh. Don't. It bores the auditors. Your preparation must be done before you enter the room. You must know what you are Fighting For. You must know the action of your first line. You must be familiar with all your lines and have your first line memorized.

All you have to do after greeting the auditors is begin your scene. You don't *wait* to begin a scene in real life. Suppose you are in a grocery store thinking about giving a piece of your mind to your nasty neighbor, who's keeping you awake every night with loud music. Suddenly you see your neighbor in the next aisle. You don't rush up to him and take deep breaths, exhale several times, crack your knuckles, and flex your muscles to relax. No. You run over and tell him what you think.

16. If you have to hit your partner during an audition, just slap his arm. It makes a nice impact and doesn't hurt. Or shake his sleeve. Make sure you check it out with your partner first. If you are reading with a reader on the other side of a desk, slap the arm of your chair or just threaten to hit.

17. You can safely ignore all stage directions. Many stage directions are put in by the stage manager to indicate what the actors did in a specific performance and are not the author's ideas. Often the stage directions tell you to sigh or look weary, and you certainly don't want to do that. Stage directions are sometimes important, but never assume they are invariably to be followed.

18. In an audition, if you have to deal with a prop such as a cup of coffee or a cigarette, lose the prop without having to carefully put it down on an imaginary table. Too much attention to props in an audition is distracting to the auditors. They don't want to watch you holding an imaginary prop throughout the whole scene. They aren't looking for a professional mime. If you have to put a ring on your partner's finger, then indicate it more or less. If you have established

there are chairs around the room, you won't lose points if you forget where they are and walk through them.

19. At the end of your audition hold your last line for at least three full seconds before breaking, and only then look at the auditors. (If you are doing a stage performance, you also hold for a few seconds before turning to an audience and bowing.) Never indicate you thought your audition was anything less than brilliant. Don't comment on your performance. Smile, say thank you or good-bye, and then leave. Unless they gush or immediately give you the job, you will not know what they thought of you, so don't dwell on it.

Listening

Actors often fake listening. They nod their heads or they make little surprised sounds or widen their eyes. We don't believe them for a minute. Free yourself from the obligation of moving your face while you listen. You don't have to consciously show expressions of amazement or displeasure or interest. In fact, you shouldn't. If it happens naturally, that's fine.

Watch people listening. Sometimes they don't move a muscle in their faces. Only their eyes reveal their concentration. What your partner is saying should be the most riveting thing you have ever heard in your life.

If you listen with *fascination* to your partner and give him silent messages, the audience won't be aware of who has the most lines. I have proved this to my students over and over. Even though you aren't speaking, make sure your energy matches or tops your partner's. Keep making Discoveries. Hang on your partner's every word and be ready every second to interrupt, even if you don't have a line for two pages. Listen with your Fighting For and intentions in mind. You haven't given up what you want just because the other person is talking. Really hear what the other actor is saying and you'll find you *can't wait for him to stop talking so you can make your point.*

The worst thing you can do while your partner talks is . . . wait. I watch actors *waiting* for their partners to be finished with a monologue. Their stomach muscles are not tight and they stand passively. Those actors are not ready for prime time.

Grab Attention by Starting with a Bang

It's a misconception that a good technique involves starting small so you have "somewhere to go" at the end. Not true! Start *huge* if you want. Grab the attention of the audience. Then come down to reality before starting up again. It's what we do in life. Get ridiculously dramatic about some issue and then realize how stupid you're being and apologize with a smile. You can scream and rant and rave and then, realizing you are getting nowhere, attempt a more reasonable tone. A scene shouldn't necessarily be small at the beginning and dramatic at the end. It's more interesting to have your scene graph like a wild hospital heart monitor.

Imagine getting overexcited discussing politics at a party. You shout your opinions and have a great time until you notice you are making some of the other guests annoyed, so you drop your voice, you may laugh at yourself, and you may be embarrassed. You are quieter until someone makes a point you just cannot take sitting down. You leap to your feet and . . .

Imagine that your first line in a script is, "I did not have sex with your husband." You could shout this in outrage. Then you realize you have misunderstood what your partner had said (Mistake) and you giggle and sort things out. But you certainly got the attention of the audience.

Touch

There is an infinite variety of touches. One is the casual touching between a couple, or siblings, or a parent and a child. Casual leaning on each other or small pats and strokes signal a long-term relationship.

When I was an acting student, I saw a scene with two women discussing their farm, which was going bankrupt. The scene was well done with nice Beats and high stakes. During the critique someone asked if the women were lesbians. I too had thought they might be, although there was no mention of their relationship in the scene and no sexual touching. The actresses said that indeed their characters were lovers, and they had done improvisations about their relationship to make their body language reflect it. Their nonsexual touches beautifully and subtly colored the scene. (This example also illustrates the importance of doing improvisations during a rehearsal period.)

Another kind of touch is the important-event touch. The first time a lover touches you is a huge deal. Just a caress across a cheek can be momentous. A teenager at the movies reaching for the hand of his date for the first time is creating a significant event. If I put one finger on the knee of the student next to me and continued teaching, imagine how uncomfortable and important that touch would be. The student would laugh; he might ask me what I was doing. He would definitely notice and *not ignore* that finger. Often during an audition I see actors giving or receiving important-event touches without acknowledging them. You don't have to *look* at the part of your body being touched—that often appears fake—but you certainly have to be aware of every touch.

> **TIP:** *Never touch or be touched without noticing it and giving it significance.*

Interrupt Yourself

If you have a line that is going to be interrupted by another actor, don't wait for that actor to interrupt you. It will never happen, unless you rehearse it over and over. In an audition you can't count on a reader to interrupt you. Make sure you don't do the amateur actor thing of trailing off unnaturally and waiting for the other actor to take over. Don't ad-lib words to fill out the thought. *We often stop a sentence in mid-thought.* We may need to think up a word, or we get distracted, or we forget what we are saying. Pick one of these choices and make it work in order to look professional.

For example, in *Sideways*, by Alexander Payne and Jim Taylor, Miles is talking to his ex-wife, Vickie, whom he still loves. She is engaged to someone else. Miles says he thought there was still some hope for their relationship, and his speech ends with two repetitions of "I just…".

After the first *I just*, abruptly stop and think hard about how to fill out the thought. Take your time. Then begin all over with a new thought, which might take you in a completely new direction. For the second *I just*, think about what you want to say with as much effort and concentration as you did the first time.

Telephones

When you have a role in which you have to be talking to someone on the phone, take more time than you would think to take at first. Give the imaginary person enough time to talk. Relax and don't rush the conversation. Get someone to watch you to see if you are rushing.

> TIP: *Do not gaze at the phone after you hang up.* Only actors do this. It's fake. After you hear terrible news over the phone you might stare straight ahead to absorb it or you may go into frantic mode to do something about it. You do not look at the phone. It is fake and what I call "actor-shmactor."

Drinking out of a Bottle

Only actors take swigs from a liquor bottle. Even the most ardent alcoholics use a glass. Of course there are exceptions, but too many actors think it makes them seem more desperate if they drink from a bottle. It doesn't. It makes them unbelievable.

What to Do When a Casting Director or a Director Tells You to "Take it Down"

If you let it, this phrase will *destroy your performance*. "Oh no! I'm overacting. They don't believe me!" Your instinct is to lose all your energy and jettison your preparation. The director is left with a pale shadow of the person he was working with and everyone is miserable. Don't throw out everything you were doing!

First, realize that great directors or casting directors don't use this phrase. Their directions are much more helpful and specific.

Second, don't lose your intensity or what you are Fighting For, or you will become small, dull, and polite, and wonder why you didn't get hired.

There are several ways to accomplish what the director is looking for.

1. Lower your volume. Perhaps you are simply too loud for the space.
2. Find your vulnerability in the scene. Becoming vulnerable to your partner will automatically soften you.

3. Perhaps you're not grounded. Reconnect with what you're Fighting For. Use *yourself* in the situation. Find the humor in the scene. Laugh at yourself. Apologize in the role for being too loud.

A talented singer belting out a song will command the attention of an audience; the same singer using the same energy but performing softly can create a feeling of intimacy and enthrall the audience just as much.

Don't *ever* lose your intensity and inner energy. *Never* change or water down your choices.

If a Director Gives You a Line Reading

Do not imitate the director! If you do, you won't sound like yourself. Try to understand what the director is getting at, and then change what he wants into an action or Fighting For. For example, if the director angrily says the line "Are you coming in, or are you going out?" don't imitate him. In this case you might translate his line reading into Fighting to intimidate your partner. Then the line becomes a believable action, not a poor imitation.

Directors are not supposed to give line readings. They're supposed to give helpful suggestions based on actions. But they get stressed. There is a lot of pressure on directors to bring the film in on time, and sometimes they must use a shorthand. I've directed films and I know how to talk to actors, but sometimes I've been so harried on the set that giving line readings was instinctive and unavoidable. Fortunately, no actor ever fell into the trap of *just* imitating me.

Questions

When you have a line with a question such as "Huh?" or "What?" or "Hmm?" never say it as if you have not heard your partner. What a boring choice. What writer would put in a *What?* for no good reason? Instead use the line to delay answering, or avoid answering, or to take time to think. There will be subtext and higher stakes in your question. Take a Beat before you say "What?"

Never ask a rhetorical question. Always wait a fraction of a second (Beat) for the answer from your partner, before you understand that you will not get one. Only then do you go on with your lines. That Beat adds tension to the scene.

Whispering

If you have to whisper (unless you are trying to be extra quiet), give the whisper some voice, not just air, so it is strong and energetic. Imagine being furious at your partner just outside a room full of people. Don't *just* whisper; use your stomach muscles and your diaphragm, so your whisper is coming from your body and not just your mouth.

Lying

Don't signal to the audience that you are lying. In life we lie like experts. "Susan, those pants fit you perfectly!"

TIP: Always lie brilliantly.

Know the Lingo

There are lots of words, terms, and titles exclusive to acting in film and stage. If you know these terms you will look professional.

Sides. These are the lines taken from the script to be used for your audition.

Upstage and **downstage**. In the old days, stages were slanted so the back was higher than the front. (Downstage is nearer the audience.)

Stage right and **stage left** are from the point of view of the actor on the stage facing the audience. A director might say, "Go upstage left of your partner."

The **Fourth Wall** is the imaginary wall on a stage. It is the "wall" between you and the audience. You should put all the stage objects such as mirrors and doors against this wall so, for example, as you put on makeup, you look in the imaginary mirror. This keeps you facing forward so the audience can see you.

Slate. *To* **slate** means to say your name (and often your agency name; you can ask) before you begin your taped audition. Slate looking directly into the camera lens. *A* **slate** is the board on which the scenes and takes are recorded by the script supervisor before each take.

Call time is the time you are due to arrive at the location.

Craft service is the snack food on a **set**, which is where a scene is being filmed. The craft service area is a place to gather and chat. Craft service is a full-time job for someone. There is always plenty of food.

It's a wrap means filming is finished for that day and you can go home.

Magic hour is the time outside at dusk or dawn when the lighting is perfect and the crew must hurry to finish a scene before the special light disappears.

Lunch is the meal served six hours after call time. That means you could have lunch at two in the morning. Except on really low-budget films, **lunch** is an elaborate catered meal with choices of entrées.

Meat puppets or **props that eat** are the terms often used by crews for the extras. (Not very nice, but I hope you're laughing.)

Make the day means to finish all the shots scheduled for that day.

Camera Terms

Master shot is the wide shot that covers the entire action and includes all the characters.

Two shot is when the camera includes two people. Usually the lens is fairly tight on the faces, but not necessarily. You should ask how tight the shot will be.

Close-up or **CU** is a very tight shot of one person's face. Every eye movement or anything you do with your mouth is exaggerated, so don't do anything not related to the scene work. You may be asked to do a master, a two shot, and a close-up for the same scene to give the editor options.

Inserts are shots of a hand or a vase or anything that is talked about or is of interest to the story. For example, if a nurse is giving a shot, an insert could be the needle going into the skin. Or an insert could be a cup of coffee on a table, or a divorce paper, or an abandoned shoe. Inserts are valuable to editors because they give an opportunity to emphasize an action or a point. Inserts also allow editors to cut away from the main action to manipulate time and space, to cut out dialogue and action, or to expand or shorten time. For example, if an editor wants to cut out some dialogue he can go to an insert and then back to the characters without the action seeming to jump.

Handheld means the camera is not propped on **sticks** but is held by the camera operator, who follows the action. The handheld motion gives another dimension to the scene.

POV stands for point of view. It is what the camera shows of the point of view of a character.

Shot List

A shot list is all the shots the director wants to get of a scene. Following is the shot list for the first scene of a film I directed called *Rockheads*. The action covered a transient sitting by a shopping cart in an alley playing idly with her chewing gum, which I asked her to roll into balls and then put the balls on a can of Healthy Choice soup in her cart. Then she hears a loud noise and a body falls onto a car next to her in the alley. She jumps up and looks at the body. She sees a suitcase full of money spilled on the ground. She looks up at the office building above her to see if anyone is looking down. She talks briefly to the dying man, who tells her to take the money and run. She grabs the money, puts it in the cart, and runs down the alley.

The following is the actual shot list we needed to cover this much action. Actors should understand what it takes to cover such a complicated scene and should be prepared to do the scene over and over from different angles.

Shot List Of Scene One

1. CU (Close up) of Tessie pulling apart gum widens to master.
2. CU of Tessie.
3. Tessie's POV (point of view) of the building with no one in the windows.
4. Tessie's POV, handheld, of Man on Car.
5. CU of Man on Car and his lines.
6. Tessie's POV of money on the ground.
7. Tessie running down alley. Wide shot. Then picking up speed. Then turning to look back.
8. Medium shot of Tessie running down the alley, turning to look back and picking up speed.

Inserts

Hand rolling gum into balls.

Money spilling out of briefcase.

Hand putting rolled gum on a can half-filled with gum balls.

Hand putting gum on a can almost full of gum balls (to show passage of time).

This scene was completed about three hours from the call time of 8:30 A.M. This time included makeup, camera, sound setup, and rehearsals.

VO stands for voice-over. It is a voice recorded in a studio and imposed over a scene. In the script it will appear as OS (off screen).

ADR is when actors re-record dialogue in a studio they have already said on the set. It is called **looping**. Sometimes the sound from the set is not usable. Actors have to match the movement of their lips with their performance.

A **Dolly** is a platform that looks like a little car. The camera is mounted on the dolly, which is operated by a **dolly grip**. It can be operated on any surface, but often it is raised onto tracks to create a moving shot.

"Flash" is what you say when you are taking a flash still picture on the set so the crew doesn't think a light has blown.

Montage is a series of shots. If a woman is getting dressed there might be a shot of her putting on her shoes, a shot of her putting on a hat, then lipstick, and so on. A montage could be of a happy couple eating in a restaurant, kissing on the beach, walking in the park holding hands. Montages are used to speed up an action like getting dressed or falling in love. Montages are not one continuous action.

Cut to is a script note that means going from one scene to another abruptly.

Fade in and **fade out** are film terms. For example, you can have a couple kissing and then it fades out and they are in bed. You can fade in to a child being brought into a classroom for the first time; then you fade out, and the next shot is the child happily playing in the schoolyard.

Monitor: A monitor is a screen like a television set the director can look at after a take to see if the action is what he wants.

Above the line means all the people who get a credit in the front of the film—producers, directors, writers, and actors.

Below the line are the heads of all the departments and their crews. Their credits come after the film.

Titles

Director: You would think at least actors would know what the director does, but one "name" actress surprised me. One day on the set I called, "Cut," because she wasn't going far enough in an emotional scene. When I talked to her about her performance, she said to me, "I won't tell you how to direct so don't tell me how to act." She was not as nasty as she sounded, but her comment showed that she didn't know what a director does, though she had worked extensively in the film business.

The director has the vision for the script. He (or she, but women are unfairly represented in the industry) discusses with the director of photography (DP) what the film should look like. The director might ask for dark mood lighting throughout, or a predominant color. The director decides whether the camera will be stationary in certain scenes, or handheld. The director works closely with the director of photography, but ultimately the director decides the look of the film and how to move the camera.

The director also signs off on the costumes, the sets, the locations, and even the makeup. When I was an actress I played Cat Mama in a Mel Brooks film. We were a futuristic family, half-cat and half-human (our part was later cut). Mel Brooks came into the makeup trailer and said only three words when he saw me. "She looks grotesque." A friend told me I should have answered that he didn't look so hot either, but the point is the director is responsible for every aspect of the film, even the makeup.

In films, the director hires most of the crew through his DP or his production manager. Often crews have worked on many films together. Clint Eastwood is known for his loyalty to his crews. His production designer for *Million Dollar Baby* is in his nineties. In television, the crew usually works together all the time, and only the directors and some actors are new each episode.

The director is responsible, with the help of the casting director, for auditioning and hiring actors, although the producers may impose actors on the director. The director is responsible for getting the performances out of the actors that he wants. But often directors come from a background of editing or producing and they may have no formal training in working with actors. Some directors ask for a lot of rehearsals, and if you get a director like that, thank your lucky stars. Some directors like to use improvisation. Others expect the actors to be ready to perform with no rehearsal, just a run-through for blocking. Often there is little flexibility for an actor on the set to try out ways of doing the scene. Usually the blocking is set, and you as the actor have to make it look spontaneous and natural. If you have one of the directors who does not rehearse, you'd better be ready to deliver a full performance the first time you meet.

Possibly the hardest thing for a director is bringing the film in on time and on budget. No one wants to hire a director who costs the producers money, and time is money. Lots of money. So never hold up a shoot. It is unforgivable.

The worst thing you can do as an actor is to be unprepared, to not know your lines or to prevent the director from making his day (finishing all the shots that were planned for the day).

In order to be on time most directors will create **storyboards**, which are pictures like cartoons of each shot and each angle planned in advance.

Director of photography (DP): In concert with the director, the DP is responsible for the camera work and the lighting. The DP is the head of the lighting and grip crews. There isn't one person on the set who isn't essential.

Grips work with the lights and also do **rigging**, which is putting cameras and lights where they are needed. For example, in *Spiderman II* they rigged seventeen cameras on the side of a train. The famous director John Huston said he would rather have a grip on a desert island with him than any other professional, because grips are innovative and excellent problem solvers.

The **Gaffer** is the head electrician, and he sets all the lighting.

Sound: There is a crew to make the sound. Bad sound can ruin a film. The head of the sound crew has headphones and hears everything. The second man makes sure everyone has headsets to listen to the monitor. Make sure that if you have a microphone on, you do not say or do anything you don't want heard, because the sound people hear everything you say. *If you need to go to the bathroom, ask to have the mike taken off.*

The **boom operator** holds the sound recording device on a long pole over the heads of the actors, out of sight of the camera.

Craft service: These are the people who provide snacks for the crew all day. It is a bigger job than it sounds, and they have long hours. The craft service table is often where people hang out when they are not working.

The **set decorator** dresses the set; the **set designer** is responsible for the look of the entire production.

The **prop master** deals with all the props.

The **costumer** will handle jewelry and hats and gloves and shoes, but if you wear a brace for the film, the prop master will be in charge of it.

The **script supervisor** keeps the records of everything shot that day. She marks what the slate says. She keeps all the takes separate for the editor. She makes notes on what takes the director likes. She also has her eye on the script for dropped lines or actions that don't match. If you have your right hand on the table for one take, she will make sure you have it on the table for all the shots.

PAs are **production assistants**. They do all the errands. They often end up as producers, so be nice to them.

The **assistant director (AD)** is like the foreman of the set, and he organizes the schedule. He makes sure the set is quiet before the director calls "Action." The AD directs the extras, but never the actors.

Transportation: Drivers are responsible for taking the equipment to the set and for driving the stars to and from the set.

Set Etiquette

It will make you feel comfortable to know how to conduct yourself on a set. Someone who knows as much about it as anyone is Twink Caplan, an experienced actor/producer, whom you may know as the teacher, Miss Geist, from the film *Clueless*. She has this advice for actors:

> Etiquette on a film set is crucial. You may hear the unspoken rules a million times and still need to refresh them in your head.
>
> Your agent calls—you got the part! You are excited and call everyone you know in North America. When your script is delivered to your house that evening, check to see if your dialogue has changed. When the Third AD phones to give you a call time and directions to the set, use the opportunity to get his/her cell phone number in case you get lost. Go fill your car with gas. Lay out your clothes for the morning, put your license, passport, or social security card in your bag, and go to sleep.
>
> If you are fortunate enough to be picked up by transportation, *be on time*. Even better, be outside! Transportation works hard. They leave their homes before your alarm clock rings and they are the last to get home in the evening. Be nice to them (they have petty

cash!). When you're on time and likable they may stop at Starbucks and get you a coffee on the way to the set. If you are five minutes late for a driver in the morning, he/she is already on the phone to the set telling everyone you're not ready. If the driver is being kind and says you can smoke, don't. There will be other people in the car that day who will smell the smoke you left, and that's a drag. Don't bring food into their vehicles. Don't gossip. You don't know who is sitting behind you in a car. Oh, and don't use deodorant or cologne to replace a shower. Nothing is worse than a smelly actor!

Arrive with clean hair, a clean face, no makeup. Girls, bring button-down shirts or wide-collar sweaters. I love to be comfy in the makeup/hair chairs in the a.m., but we must be able to take the shirts off easily and not screw with their work and the time it took them to give us "big" hair or whatever.

When you arrive on set, find the First Assistant Director and introduce yourself. The AD will direct you to your trailer and alert the costume department to bring in your clothes. Stay in the trailer until someone tells you to go to the makeup/hair department.

Don't complain about anything they have given you to wear even if you think it makes you look like Eleanor Roosevelt.

In the makeup trailer try to stay quiet. If the stars are sitting in the next chairs, wait for them to talk to you. They will be focused on their lines and don't need interruptions.

Don't add makeup or even sunblock after the artist does your face. She will know if you added mascara on the last eyelash from 15 yards away. The makeup artist and hairdresser have talked to the director, who has told them how he/she wants you to look. Believe me, they've discussed your look down to the lipstick or hair gel.

Don't play with your hair after the hairdresser has set it. Guys do that more than girls. They rake their fingers through the top of their hair as if they are worried they're going bald. What is it with younger men?

When you're on set don't tell the story of your life, embellish your credits, or tell about your experiences as an extra with George Clooney. Really. It's tedious and boring to hear actors mumbling while the Director is concentrating on setting up the shot with the Director of Photography. The worst is having the First AD turn and scream "Shut up!" in your direction. (The First AD's job is to keep the set calm and quiet).

When you're quiet you can listen and learn. You can take in the information—where the camera will be, what angle, and what they are going for in the scene.

Don't ever have a cell phone or a computer on set and *no photo ops*. With TMZ and the gossip rags, everyone is paranoid. If you have a camera, keep it in your trailer. Take a picture of yourself in costume so you can send it to your mother, but don't take it on the set!

Remember: You never know who someone might be, so smile and respect every person on the set.

And one more thing—I know it's free food and we all love free food, but act first, eat later. Eating too much can make you lethargic.

Make sure you sign out before you leave, and get your ID back! Also, hang your costumes on hangers the way you received them, put the jewelry back in the plastic bag, and don't take home the stockings or anything they have given you. Check the bathroom and make sure everything is neat and clean the way you found it.

After you leave the set, the costume department has to go into everyone's trailers and tidy up. The drivers have to empty the bathrooms and clean up. Make their jobs easier and they will remember you.

I always feel lucky to be around a movie or television set. Make friends. Enjoy the ride!

Summary

An excellent technique must be second nature to a professional actor.

Until your technique is perfect, you won't be free to Fight fully for what you need from your partner because you will be worrying about how to hold your script, how to stand, or when to begin.

If you have mastered the technique of acting, if you know how to work with a director, if you know your way around a set, and if you know the basics of filmmaking and the lingo, you'll never have to worry that you'll make a fool of yourself. You will appear to be what you are—a professional.

10 Questions and Answers

The following are questions I often hear from actors. I hope they are helpful.

What if my choice was wrong for the scene?

What if you were not told you were having an affair with the wife of your boss? Or what if you didn't know you were supposed to have a terminal disease? If you had a strong Fighting For anyway and if you were engaging, strong, interesting, and energetic, your wrong choice will only make the casting director want to redirect you to the correct choice. It won't necessarily hurt your chances for a call back. But always ask what the situation is if you have not had the chance to read the entire script.

I don't feel right for the part. I can't relate.

What you *feel* means nothing. Sure it's nice if you can relate to the part, and it's easy for you, but if your technique is strong and you make strong choices, the auditors won't notice.

The audition is over and I'm worried I didn't do well.

You may or may not get the part, but again how you feel you did seldom has anything to do with how you appeared to them. Often actors

207

tell me they blew the audition, and then they get hired. If you have a solid technique, you will never fall below a professional level.

I got laughs and it was a drama! Help!
If they weren't laughing because you were grossly unprepared or trailing toilet paper, then what you did was so perfect and universal that the laugh was one of acknowledgment. If you made the right choices, laughs can be the highest compliment in a drama. These laughs are totally unpredictable, so you can't plan for them.

Where do I put the person I'm talking to when I do a monologue?
Put your imaginary partner on either side of the stage with his back to the audience. Do not put him at the back of the theater, and don't use the auditors in the theater. If you are in a small room with a casting director, you may ask if you can direct the monologue to him/her.

Refer to your imaginary partner only 10 percent of the time. Look over at him once in a while to see if he is with you, or if he is getting your point. But don't feel an obligation to "see" him. No one cares.

Be sure to give the imaginary partner some height. I've watched actors look at the floor or at the seat of a chair as if their partners were microscopic.

Monologues are hell on you and on the auditors. Make them *short*—never longer than five minutes, at the most.

May I take a minute before I start?
Absolutely not. No way. Don't even think about it.

Remember, the auditors have seen twenty actors before you, and are facing twenty actors after you. They want to get home at a reasonable hour. They certainly don't want to watch you preparing. Not only does it not impress them to watch you "getting into character" (especially when you should be playing yourself in the situation) but it makes them tear their hair out with boredom.

Your preparation must be done before you enter the room. You must know how you want to change your partner. You must know the action of your first line. You must be very familiar with your lines. All your work is done when you step into the room, so all you have to do is *briefly* greet the auditors and begin your scene.

What is the difference between stage and film acting?

The difference is minimal.

Many actors have the misconception that film acting is "natural" and doesn't require the same energy as stage acting. Unfortunately, what they mean by "natural" is low energy, low voice, and "sincere."

Not true.

In theater you have an obligation to be heard in the back rows, and you have to place yourself where you will be seen by the audience, but you must be as truthful and natural as in film. The projection that is required can make actors unbelievable. Don't allow it to happen to you. Don't shout. Don't use an unnatural pitch. Just think of speaking up. That is all. On film you have to have the same focus and energy as you have on stage; you just don't have to project. You do have to use energy. Your stomach muscles have to be just as engaged. You have to be working hard to change your partner.

Don't use a fake soft voice because you are on film. It will make you look not only fake, but weak.

As far as "natural" goes—you always have to be natural. Energy is natural. You have to be you in the circumstances of the scene. Otherwise we won't believe you.

May I ad-lib or add extra words?

No. Not one extra word. It is sloppy to add "I means" and "uhs," and it is rude to the writer to add lines. Say what is written and only what is written. Don't go on if your line is interrupted. For example, if your line is, "What I mean was—" then interrupt yourself abruptly as if you can't think of what else to say. Don't wait for another actor to interrupt you, and don't add your own words.

I'm late to an audition. What should I say?

A famous casting director told me the only acceptable excuse for being late was, "I was held over at another audition." You might think in LA at least, casting directors would be sympathetic about car trouble and traffic. The truth is they don't want actors who have bad cars, and they think you should have prepared for the traffic. The simplest solution is—*never be late*. Arrive early.

If you are unavoidably late, ask the receptionist if your lateness was noticed. If it was not, don't mention it. If the answer is yes, apologize *once* calmly to the casting director (with the excuse of the last audition), as if you are not usually late, and get on with your audition. Never apologize more than once, or you will appear frazzled. Don't apologize again at the end of your audition, because the auditors may have forgotten that you were late and you don't want to remind them.

You always want to appear reliable. No one wants to lose time on the set waiting for late, irresponsible actors.

An agency is willing to represent me, but they want me to pay a fee and use their photographer for my headshots.

Never pay an agency. No reputable agency requires fees, nor will they force you to use one photographer. Walk away.

I have an audition. Should I get a professional coach?

Yes. Unless the part is tiny, you should have a coach for every audition. An excellent coach will not only help you make your audition stronger, but will also make each moment of your audition so specific that you will go moment to moment and not be nervous.

I am overweight. Will I still get work?

If you are a young leading man or woman you have to be at your ideal weight and toned. Period. If you are a character actor, extra weight can get you work. In either case, be fit and at your best.

I have to kiss my partner and he/she is unattractive. How can I do it convincingly?

Something that may help is to look into your partner's eyes and see the little child who was once there. You can love that child. You can feel compassion, and that is a positive emotion you can build on.

If nothing works, then act "as if" you are attracted. Filmed sex scenes are usually done in pieces, and there is most often no real excitement, not with the entire crew watching. So act enthusiastic and it will look enthusiastic.

Should I memorize my audition piece?

If you have time, it will make you more comfortable to memorize it. But even if you know it cold, hold your script and refer to it now and then. In Australia they give you time to memorize and actors don't hold their scripts, but in the United States, if you don't hold the script, the auditors might expect much more from you—a polished performance. Also, the auditors are used to actors holding scripts at auditions. You don't want them to be wondering why you are not holding yours.

What if I don't have anything important on my résumé?
If you are young, being green could be an advantage. Get into an excellent class and become the best actor you can. Casting directors don't mind discovering you. Get tape of yourself as soon as possible by getting into student or low-budget films. Join showcases to show off your talent. This business is all about whom you know, so start networking. Send out mass mailings. Get an excellent picture and résumé and find innovative ways to get them out. Use every single contact you have. Every day you should do several things toward getting yourself known. Every single day.

I was offered a job in a play but it is not good. Should I do it anyway and hope someone sees me?
No. Work as much as possible, but not in bad productions. Actors are so anxious to work that I have seen them lose all perspective and appear in terrible plays, which do them more harm than good. Casting directors don't often go to plays anyway. You will be wasting your time in rehearsals and in performances that no one comes to see, and if people do come they will only associate you with a bad production.

My director is not being helpful. I worry that he doesn't know what he is doing. How should I handle this?
Lots of directors have no idea how to talk to actors or what makes a scene work from an acting point of view. Film directors often were former editors or even ADs. Sometimes they are producers who got the money together. The answer is to protect yourself by being very prepared. Know your craft so well that you come up with the entire performance. Don't expect to be molded. Directors choose actors to make themselves look good.

I'm on the set and I have a great idea for an extra line or some blocking or a movement. May I suggest it to the director?
If the director makes it easy for you to suggest things, go ahead. Some directors are open to ideas. But if you sense your comments are not

being well received, stop immediately. The pressure and stress and sheer physical work of directing all combine to exhaust directors. Make it easy for your director to want to work with you again. You may suggest ways to play a scene, but the director's word is final. Don't give any "helpful" suggestions that will slow down the shoot, or the crew will have you for breakfast.

The director only gives suggestions to my partner. I feel ignored. What is going on?

You're getting a big compliment. The director is happy with your performance. Directors don't always remember to praise actors. They forget what an insecure bunch of people most actors are.

How old should I say I am?

You are the age of the character you are playing. Age is subjective anyway, and if they want you for the part they will stretch their views of age.

If a casting director asks for your age, give an age range only. *Never* tell your real age. It pigeonholes you. To get your age range I usually recommend taking your real age and subtracting five years. If you are twenty-five, your age range is from twenty to twenty-five. If you look young, go younger. Youth sells. Casting directors particularly like actors who look like teens but are older than eighteen, so no one has to get involved in the many rules about minors.

I have trouble memorizing. What should I do?

Often actors don't do the work that thorough memorizing entails. You must not think you have a piece memorized unless you work on it over a long period, till the words become second nature. Then even when you forget them because of nerves, your mouth will say them for you. This doesn't happen overnight.

As soon as you get a part, start saying your lines out loud with no expression. It is important that your ears hear the words and your mouth forms them over and over. I suggest taking your script into your car and saying your lines aloud as you drive.

If you don't work on memorizing long enough, the words will fly out of your head when you get on the set or on a stage and become stressed.

My reader in the audition gave me nothing and talked in a whisper. What should I have done?

Act "as if" the reader gave you as much as you wanted. Lots of casting directors think it is a good idea to just murmur responses. I think they should find professional actors to read with you, but in any case don't let their low energy affect you. Make the strong, intense, risky choices I recommend, or you won't get the job.

I know I am not right for the part. Should I audition anyway?

Of course. You should be seen as much as you can. I remember the auditions of outstanding actors for years and I keep them in mind for future jobs. If you are not right for one part, you might be right for the next project or for another role.

In the audition we hand a glass back and forth. Should I use a real glass?

Never use real props for an audition. You are holding your script in any case, so it would be awkward. Also, the prop might become a focus instead of you. So use an imaginary glass and lose it when you don't need it any more. You don't have to carefully put it down on an imaginary table either. Just let it go into thin air. If you established a table in the middle of the stage, you can walk right through it. At auditions no one cares about props or your miming abilities.

I got a call back. What should I wear to the next audition?

Wear exactly what you wore for your first audition. The auditors often remember you by what you wore, so if you don't turn up in that green sweater, they won't remember you were the one who made them laugh so hard. Wear the same outfit no matter how many times you are called back until you get the job.

I have a cold and my voice is hoarse. Should I audition anyway?

Yes. You must take every opportunity to be seen. Tell the casting director only *once* about your throat. You may use your hoarseness naturally in the part by apologizing for it with a laugh or a shake of your head as you clear your throat. They will admire you for it.

I get so nervous at auditions that I can't think. What will help?

Memorize your first line and deliver it looking at your partner. If you have time, memorize the whole scene so you don't have to worry about finding the line.

If you fumble over a line, don't worry about it. We fumble in real life. *Never* apologize or grimace or comment on a fumble. Professional actors (and musicians) cover their mistakes well.

Be so specific in your rehearsal for the audition that you go from moment to moment and line to line knowing exactly what you are doing. Never try to wing an audition. Always take the time to know what you are Fighting For. Plan physical actions in advance. Know your blocking cold, although you may have to adjust for the size of the room. The more specific you are in your rehearsal and preparation, the more comfortable you will be. Take classes until your technique is perfect. Your acting skills will then carry you through any challenge. If you can afford it, get coached.

I have to wear glasses to audition but I look so ugly in them!

When you enter the room to audition, don't wear your glasses. Smile and talk briefly to the auditors so they can see you without them. Do the audition comfortably with your glasses on, although you can take them off briefly if your partner has a monologue. As soon as the audition is over, remove your glasses to say good-bye.

The character needs to have an accent. I can't get it down in one day. What should I do?

You can approximate the accent and tell the casting director you are very good with accents and will perfect it quickly if you get the part. You can also ask the casting director if you should do the part without an accent or use the approximation. If you get the part, hire a dialogue coach.

Make sure you are positive about your abilities. I once told a casting director my voice was excellent for commercials. In my call back the casting director told the producer, "This is the woman we were telling you about with the great speaking voice." I had made it up! It was the power of suggestion. You want to make the casting director have confidence in you.

How do I choose a teacher?

There is no good answer. There are so many teachers and so few good ones. I would say if you audit some classes and hear good, practical, helpful suggestions for improving your work, you are on the right track. Unless you are a beginner and need to do lots of exercises in order to feel freer, I would look for a teacher who emphasizes getting the most out of a script. A good teacher will make you risk and take chances. A good teacher has probably worked in the industry. Look for teachers who will significantly improve your work and your understanding of scripts within a few months or move on to one who is more helpful. I would not recommend teachers who talk about "character work." Good acting teachers will help you to use yourself in the situation.

I discourage actors from taking classes that are filmed because it makes them self-conscious about the way their mouth moves, or about their double chin. Self-consciousness of this kind makes actors forget all about what they are Fighting For with their partner.

I also don't recommend wasting time on "camera technique" classes. Each scene you do on the set will be different in terms of movement. If you have to hit a mark, it will be carefully explained to you and you will rehearse it. If you are sitting on a box to make you taller, the move will be rehearsed. You will be told when you are moving out of camera range. Each shot is unique, so it seems a waste of time to study "camera technique."

How do I choose a photographer?

Price is not always an indication of a good photographer. Make sure you see the photographer's work. Look for expression. A beautiful picture is nice, but unless the expression is arresting and full of energy it won't get you work. You need a picture with a great smile. You need a serious one showing lots of depth. Pretty is not enough.

In Los Angeles and New York, color photographs are now the norm.

It's odd how many actors accept pictures that are not quite in focus. Don't use a picture no matter how great it makes you look, unless it is in sharp focus.

Hire a professional makeup artist. It will make all the difference. Just make sure your picture looks like you and is not overly glamorized.

The acting business is so discouraging. Should I keep trying?

No. If you can even ask that question, go on to something else. Stay only if, in your mind, you have no other choice. The truth is that many wonderful, talented actors never make a living at it. It is one of those professions that may not pay off in fame or fortune even if you are talented, persistent, and connected. So if you love it, stay in it, but know what you're up against.

How can I get into the Screen Actors Guild?

You have to be in the Screen Actors Guild (SAG) in order to work in union films. Most agents won't represent you unless you are a member of the union. It is a catch-22 situation; you can't work (except on low-budget non-union films) unless you are union, and you can't get a union card unless you work.

There are three ways to get into SAG. 1) You have to know someone who will give you a speaking role, or you have to be lucky enough to be given a line when you are an extra. For example, you can get into SAG if you are an extra playing a priest and the director decides you need to say, "You may kiss the bride." The process of getting your SAG card from being given a line is called being "Taft Hartley-ed." It costs the production money. Then you have to pay the union entrance fees, which are substantial. 2) You must have been a member for at least a year and have worked at least once as a principal player in an affiliated union such as AFTRA or AGVA or Equity. 3) You can work as an extra and get three SAG vouchers to qualify you for membership. This is a hard process because films and commercials and television productions have to hire a certain number of union extras. Only if you are fortunate enough to be on a production that requires more than that number will you, a non-union extra, pick up a SAG voucher. It helps to make friends with the extra casting people or producers. Good luck!

I just broke up with my boyfriend. I am miserable and crying and my call time is tomorrow.

Don't tell one person about it on the set. Be cheerful. Do not indulge your emotions. Be professional and don't even think about allowing your eyes to be red from crying. (You'll find another boyfriend.)

I am sick and my call time is tomorrow. What should I do?
There is no such thing as being sick. The show must go on. I know an actress who was called when she was feverish with flu. When some of the crew heard her raspy voice and asked if she was okay, she dismissed it by telling them she had a sinus condition. Another actress did her scenes as she was passing a kidney stone, and no one knew. You are either serious about this business or you are not. Don't make a big thing out of being sick. Do your job. Don't cause problems. Time is money.

I'm on the set and we're running late. I am going to be late for my job as a bartender. What should I do?
To professional actors this is a ridiculous question, but I can't tell you how many times I have heard about actors in small productions needing to "get home." First of all, understand that filmmaking takes a long time. It runs over very often. You should not expect to get home ten, twelve, or even sixteen hours after you are called. Plan to be called a day later than scheduled if the director falls behind. You have to clear your schedule. No matter how small the film or project you are doing, *never* bother the director with your problems. You are either an actor or a bartender. It is up to you to choose. No director will hire any actor again who has temperament problems or gives any trouble whatsoever unless that actor is a "name." Never show any anger, any needs, or demand special attention. If you have a sore throat, hide it. If you break your leg, keep going. If you faint, fan yourself and get up and do the next take. Time is crucial on a set. Time is big money to the producers. Falling behind can be a career-breaker for a director. Repeat: there should be no attitude, no personal crises, and no sickness on a set. You are now a professional.

A Manual on How to Rehearse

by Michael Shurtleff, author of *Audition*

Michael Shurtleff was my teacher for more than seven years. I took his classes in New York City and in Los Angeles. At first I was so terrified of him that I cowered in the back until he said, "Deryn, are you just going to sit there or actually do a scene?" After years of his instruction, I began teaching his class when he was away, something I could never have envisioned that first day. I owe my career in film directing and teaching to him. He was my fascinating and close friend until his death.

After reading this book and giving me suggestions, he also gave me the gift of using his manual on rehearsing, which has never before been published. If there is anything in his instructions that is not clear to you, read his famous book, *Audition*, a classic that most actors use as their bible.

A Manual on How to Rehearse

by Michael Shurtleff

"A Manual on How to Rehearse" throws emphasis on how to take care of yourself, because the reality of both film and television acting is that most of the time you are on your own, either with little or no direction or with direction given to you entirely in terms of results. An actor in television or films must learn to achieve those results immediately. When the camera is ready, the actor has to be ready. The aim of our Scene Study Workshop is to teach you how to be ready.

This means you have to learn how to work on your own, without the director, without the other actor, even without rehearsal time. You have to learn how to make specific choices quickly and economically, which means you must be able to draw on your own life and emotions readily.

Since the art of acting is the art of creating relationships, use your workshop rehearsal time fully to learn how to work with real people in a real rehearsal process—so that you will know what to do when there is no rehearsal process and you meet the other actor for the first time in front of the camera.

Here is one essential difference between stage and screen acting: the camera picks up what you think. A good screen actor is one who is *always thinking* (which is the communication of feelings through silent dialogue) and whose thoughts are always specific.

Don't believe that screen acting is "taking it down" or "making it subtle." You need the same life-force important impulses that you need for stage acting, so the adjustment you make is *only* because of the physical proximity of the camera: the person you are relating to is right next to you, lying in bed with you or sitting so close to you on the sofa you can actually feel the warmth of their body.

How to Rehearse
  1. Reading the script.
     Don't start to read from the point of innocence. Instead start to read, *for the first time*, from having this foreknowledge: This is going to be about me involved in a love relationship.

Ask: What do I want? What am I fighting *for* in this love relationship? And what gets in my way? What interferes with my getting what I *need*? This is *finding the conflict*.

At the same time, find the *opposites* of what you are fighting *for*. As an example—if you are fighting to create a love relationship with the other person in the script, then the opposite is wanting to be independent, to be strong enough not to need a relationship so you can stand on your own two feet.

So do not come to the first rehearsal with your partner with an open mind, ready to read through the play with a "Let's see what this is about" attitude. Come to it prejudiced, with your mind made up about:

- What you are fighting for in this relationship
- What creates the conflict
- What the opposite is

Remember: the opposite of having your mind made up is having an open mind to changes based on new information you may find out. This might lead you to make a more *basic*, therefore deeper, choice, and will also allow you to add many *different ways* of expressing what you are fighting for.

Figure out in advance what your partner in the scene is fighting for. Then find out in the first rehearsal what your fellow actor has decided he is fighting for. Remember: *you do not have to agree on what you are fighting for. In life, people don't agree*—and they manage to have scenes together all the time!

2. Don't talk; do.
There's far too much talking and analyzing in the usual rehearsal process. One improvisation is worth ten discussions.

When I ask, where is a missing element in the scene, actors tell me, "We talked about that," which proves that talking about it doesn't get it into the performance.

Do It. Put what you're talking about into the scene. If it doesn't happen in the rehearsal, then improvise to make sure it is there.

Improvising is one of the most important elements in the rehearsal process. Improvise about the *past*, about what happened in earlier incidents between the two of you. Improvise about the *future*, about what you *wish* could happen; about what you *fear* may happen.

Rules about improvising:

Seek confrontations, rather than avoid them.

Operate on needing something *now* and refuse to postpone your need.

Once you face a confrontation, seek to explore its consequences, which will then lead to another confrontation.

Insist on making events happen. An event is where there is new knowledge that creates a change in a relationship.

3. At your second rehearsal, read the scene together a different way. Read the line as written; then, before your partner responds with his line as written, say aloud what you are really thinking and feeling.
   Proceed through the entire scene this way.
   If you get stuck later on in the rehearsal process, do this method of reading the play again. This method, like improvising, is better than discussing and analyzing the script: it is another way of *doing* rather than talking.

4. Play Ping-Pong.
   Most scenes are too slow. They are much slower than the usual life pace.
   Therefore, every third run-through you do with your partner should be an effort to add the game of Ping-Pong to what you are doing in the scene.

Think of what the game of Ping-Pong means:

It means immediate response: return the serve or you lose.

It means there's no time to stop to think: you have to respond immediately.

It means expressing joy when you win and dismay when you lose. It also means willingness to express admiration when your partner does well. This *score-keeping* is an important element in anyone who plays the game well. No one likes to play with someone who won't revel in the wins and losses.

Ping-Pong doesn't mean just going faster (although picking up cues always helps); it means making the stakes higher and more important.

5. At each rehearsal, explore and add two more of the Guideposts (which you will find explained in *Audition* in the section called the Twelve Guideposts):

The Moment Before

Humor

Discoveries

Communication and Competition

Life and Death Importance

Find the Events

Use the Place

Game Playing and Role Playing

Mystery and Secret

6. Humor is the most essential ingredient in any relationship, and it is the one most often left out by actors.

The more serious the stakes, the more necessary it is to find humor.

Find humor in every scene, in every event, in every relationship.

7. The Moment Before is what you start with. Therefore it is important that it be *specific* and emotionally charged so that it will throw you into the scene to accomplish what you are fighting for.

Don't ever start any rehearsal or *performance* without re-creating your Moment Before. What you do in the Moment Before will affect every moment you do in the scene.

8. Conflicts and problems will normally occur between actors working on a scene. Expect them; they are not unusual.

   The only solution to conflicts and problems is the determination to keep communicating.

   There is a tendency to pile up injustices, to become a collector of injustices. This is easy to do. The hard thing is to keep communicating even when you'd like to kill your partner or the director. Even when you feel you're not being dealt with fairly, even when you feel your partner isn't communicating at all, you must keep the channels open. Listen. Be willing to hear what the opposite side's view really is; be willing to consider it

   es determination and skill.
   d them for every scene you

   de of the rehearsal process, so
   n it comes time to rehearse

   iey don't really work outside
   y "think" about the scene: do
   idepost questions; *write down*

   your own life.

   Don't limit your choices and feelings to your concrete everyday realistic life: always tap your fantasy life as well.

10. If you only rehearse the words of the script, then you haven't explored the relationship between your life and the life of the script.

    Don't go to the first rehearsal like an empty blackboard ready to be written on. Go to the first rehearsal with half your rehearsal work already done: start out way ahead of the game.

    There's a highly prevalent but mistaken conception that an actor should come to the first rehearsal with an "open mind."

An open mind in this case just means you haven't done your preliminary work. Instead, come to the first rehearsal filled with decisions and prejudices, with your mind made up. Only then can you be open to changes that are worthwhile.

11. Think of the difference between stage and screen acting this way: on stage, your partner is always on the other side of the stage; in screen acting, your partner is right next to you.

12. TAKE RISKS. Safe acting is dull acting. Learn to take risks. Learn to make every situation one that has life-and-death stakes.

    Taking risks is not a separate operation. Take risks in *every* guidepost you apply to your scene. Do *more* than you would in ordinary life. Do *more* than you think you should.

13. Learn to physicalize all your choices. Even if you end up in a small office doing your audition, or even if you end up in a tiny set squeezed up close to your partner or the camera, the fact that you have conceived of the scene in *physicalized* terms will make your acting stronger, more specific, and more emotional.

    Find out always what the physical actions are that extend the emotions you are feeling. Put them into the scene.

14. Learn your lines early. The sooner you are off the book, the sooner you will (a) physicalize, (b) take risks, and (c) create relationship needs.

    Have your lines learned by the second or third rehearsal. Otherwise you'll never make it in television or film.

*E*pilogue

I hope this book has freed you to be a better actor, to take huge risks, and to use your unique, full, and fascinating self in every role.

I wish for every actor who reads this book (all the way through) that you make a killing (or at least work steadily) in this challenging profession.

—Deryn Warren

$\mathcal{P}$erformance Rights